The Economics of the American Newspaper

The ECONOMICS of the AMERICAN NEWSPAPER

by DR. JON G. UDELL
Irwin Maier Professor of Business
Graduate School of Business
The University of Wisconsin

and CONTRIBUTING AUTHORS

Publication Sponsored by
American Newspaper Publishers
Association Foundation
Reston, Virginia

COMMUNICATION ARTS BOOKS
Hastings House, Publishers New York 10016

This book is dedicated to the many newspaper men and women who have contributed their talent and devoted their lives to the creation, production and distribution of strong, free newspapers in America's strong and democratic society.

Copyright © 1978
by American Newspaper Publishers
Association Foundation

All rights reserved. No part of this publication may be reproduced, stored in a retrieval system, or transmitted, in any form or by any means, electronic, mechanical, photocopying, recording or otherwise, without the prior permission of the copyright owner or the publishers.

Library of Congress Cataloging in Publication Data

Udell, Jon G
   The economics of the American newspaper.

   (Communication arts books)
   Includes bibliographical references and index.
   1. Newspaper publishing—Economic aspects—United States. I. Title.
PN4734.U3   338.4'7'0713   77-14492
ISBN 0-8038-1932-3
ISBN 0-8038-1933-1 pbk.

Published simultaneously in Canada by Copp Clark, Ltd., Toronto
Printed in the United States of America

Contents*

Acknowledgments	7
About the Authors	9
Preface	11
1. **The Economics of American Democracy**	13

Birth of the American System—Our Economic System—Individualism—Consumer Choice in a Free Market—Competition—The Profit Motive—The Rule of Government

2. **Economic Status of U.S. Newspapers**	23

Social Significance of Newspapers—Number of Newspapers—A Major Employer—Newspaper Income—Newspaper Advertising—Circulation—Newspaper vs. National Growth—A Recent Decade

3. **The Marketing Concept and Newspaper Organization**	40

Marketing and the Marketing Concept—Challenge of the Press—Newspapers Serve Two Markets—How Editors Try to Determine Reader Interests—How Circulators Try to Determine What Readers Want—Advertising, The Second Newspaper Market—State of Newspaper Marketing Today—Newspaper Organization and the Marketing Concept—Where the Newspaper Functions—How the Newspaper Functions—The Case for Consensus—The

*Footnotes are at the end of each chapter.

Importance of the Editorial Function—Advertising is Also a Reader Service—What the Advertising Department Sells—Advertising's Contribution to the Editorial Department—Circulation's Contribution to the Newspaper—Completing the Structure—Alternative Views

4. **Understanding Profit in the Newspaper Business** — 64
The Profit Controversy—The Role of Profit—Blessings and Evils of Profit—Explanations of Profit—Profit: A Cost—The Profitability of Newspapers—Return on Equity—Are Newspaper Profits "Reasonable"?—Profit Problems of the Press—The Trend Toward Public Ownership—Group Ownership

5. **Quality, Price and Planning** — 80
Elements of a Quality Newspaper—News Content—Features—Opinion—Advertising—Physical Appearance—Delivery Service—Community Involvement—Pricing a Quality Product—Planning and Budgeting—Monitoring Performance

6. **The Dynamics of Newspaper Production** — 88
The Publishers' Decision—The Evolutionary Revolution: First, Offset—The Newspaper Production Process: Old and New—The Traditional Letterpress System—The New System—Capital Requirements of the Modern Newspaper

7. **Anatomy of Newspaper Revenues** — 99
Circulation Revenue—Independent Distributors—Circulation Revenue Trends—Pricing Practices—Circulation Trends—Effect of Prices on Circulation—Current Problems and Opportunities—Advertising Revenue—Revenue Related to Market—Advertising Revenue and Circulation—Revenue and Management Policies—Competition is Severe—Classification of Newspaper Advertising—Preprints—Local Retail Advertising—National Advertising—Classified Advertising

8. **Newspaper Costs and Control** — 117
Goals of Cost Control—The Nature of Newspaper Costs—Controllable Costs—Problems in Controlling Costs—Cost Control Strategies—Editorial Costs—Newsprint Costs—Personnel Costs and Productivity—Measurability—Communications and Coordination—Contingency Planning

9. **Employe Relations in the Newspaper Business** — 131
Unionization—Importance of Employe Relations—Newspapers Are Labor Intensive—Is Compensation Adequate?—Effective Collective Bargaining—"People Power" Planning—Employe Benefits—Communication

10. **The Newspaper of the Next Decade** — 144
The Technological Horizon—The Physical Product—Advertising and Competition—News-Editorial Competition—Distribution—Newsprint Supply—Economics—Newspaper Employes—A Long-Term Economic Threat

Index — 156

Acknowledgments

THE AUTHOR is deeply indebted to the American Newspaper Publishers Association Foundation. Special appreciation is due to its current and past Trustees, Officers and staff, as well as to the many members of the American Newspaper Publishers Association who reviewed chapters and provided valuable suggestions.

Also greatly appreciated is the Irwin Maier Chair of Business program of the Graduate School of Business at the University of Wisconsin—Madison. Without the financial support of the ANPA Foundation and this program, *The Economics of the American Newspaper* would not have been possible.

Of special significance is the assistance of the contributing authors—Laird B. Anderson, John H. Colburn, Paul S. Hirt, Francis D. Kelly, Thomas J. McCollow and Stanford Smith. Each of these experts brought a rich background of newspaper experience to the development of this book, as did copy editors Alan Horton, Richard Schroeder, Stephen E. Palmedo of ANPA Foundation, Albert W. Caron Jr. of ANPA and Jerry W. Friedheim, general manager of ANPA.

Also greatly appreciated are the excellent services of Dorothy Peterson who patiently typed many drafts of the manuscript.

J. G. U.

About the Authors

JON G. UDELL, the main author, is Irwin Maier Professor of Business at the University of Wisconsin—Madison, consulting economist for the American Newspaper Publishers Association (ANPA) and a member of the boards of directors of several public interest organizations. Dr. Udell is the author of over 100 books, research monographs and journal articles about newspapers, marketing, research methodology, economic development and the consumer.

Laird B. Anderson, assistant professor of communication and director of the print journalism program of the School of Communication at The American University of Washington, D.C., co-authored Chapter 4—Understanding Profit in the Newspaper Business.

John H. Colburn, publisher of *The Californian* in El Cajon, Calif., prepared most of Chapter 8—Newspaper Costs and Control.

Paul S. Hirt, vice president/promotion of the *Chicago Sun Times* and *Daily News,* contributed Chapter 3—The Marketing Concept and Newspaper Organization.

Francis D. Kelly, senior vice-president and business manager of Newspapers, Inc., Milwaukee, Wis., wrote much of Chapter 9—Employe Relations in the Newspaper Business.

Thomas J. McCollow, senior vice-president for finance and corporate planning of the Journal Company, Milwaukee, Wis., contributed materials in Chapters 5 and 7—Quality, Price and Planning and Anatomy of Newspaper Revenues.

Stanford Smith, past general manager of ANPA, was co-author of Chapters 6 and 10—The Dynamics of Newspaper Production and The Newspaper of the Next Decade.

Also contributing significantly to Chapter 6 was Professor Paul Jess of the University of Michigan Department of Journalism.

Preface

WHILE PUBLISHERS may find this book of interest, it is not written for them. It is written for students of journalism and communication, reporters, editors, advertising personnel, production and business managers, circulators and the many other employes essential for the successful creation, production and distribution of the American newspaper. Hopefully, it will be of interest to all who are concerned with the maintenance of a free press and an informed citizenry.

Chapter 1 concentrates on the economic environment of the free press, describing the essential role that economic rights and responsibilities play in creating and preserving press freedom and in supporting the First Amendment of our Constitution.

Chapter 2 is devoted to the economic status of U. S. newspapers since World War II. It notes that while the role of the free press in providing news is readily recognized, the economic significance of newspapers often is overlooked. As the U. S. Department of Commerce points out, "Among the (nation's) 451 manufacturing classifications, only steel mills and manufacturers of automobile parts and accessories employ more people than newspaper publishers."[1]

[1] U.S. Department of Commerce, *U.S. Industrial Outlook 1976,* Washington, D.C., January 1976, p. 297.

The third chapter emphasizes newspaper organization and the "marketing concept." Included is a discussion of the challenge to the editor to be "market" oriented while still maintaining the newspaper's integrity.

Chapter 4 is devoted to profit—an often misunderstood dimension of American economic life. It examines the role of profit in maintaining the viability and quality of a newspaper.

Economic objectives and newspaper planning are the subjects of Chapter 5, while the technology and capital requirements of newspapers are examined in the following chapter which details the major technological revolution occurring within the newspaper business.

Chapters 7 and 8, respectively, are devoted to an analysis of newspaper revenues and costs. Current developments in circulation, advertising and cost controls are examined.

The most important ingredient in a newspaper is people, and the management of people is the subject of Chapter 9.

The closing chapter looks to the immediate future—the U.S. newspaper of the next decade.

The purpose of this book is to increase understanding of the "total" daily newspaper and of how it functions; and to explore its problems and opportunities—and the role that business and economic considerations play in assuring the free public a free press.

J. G. U.

1

The Economics of American Democracy

> *Freedom is the right to choose, the right to create for oneself the alternatives of choice. Without the possibility of choice and the exercise of choice, man is but a number, an instrument, a thing.*
> —THOMAS JEFFERSON

A FREE PRESS long has been recognized as indispensable to American democracy. The First Amendment of the U.S. Constitution proclaims press freedom. This unique constitutional foundation allows the independent American press to probe fearlessly areas into which the media of most other nations may pry only timidly, if at all.

Political and economic freedom are basic to American life. Two events in 1776—the signing of the American Declaration of Independence and the appearance of *The Wealth of Nations* by a Scottish moral philosopher, Adam Smith—are landmarks in the history of man's search for freedom and a more satisfying life. This search led consistently in the direction of increased opportunity for the individual to make the choices that would determine the quality of his or her life. Freedom of individual decision making, with minimal constraints to protect the general interest, was central to both the Declaration of Independence and to Adam Smith's view of the economy.

The virtually simultaneous appearance of these two documents, one political and the other economic, underlines a basic principle of American democracy—freedom is indivisible. To deprive a person of the right to vote is also to deprive him or her of the right to decide on the kind of economic system in which he or she wishes to participate. Conversely, the power to decide how a person shall earn a livelihood can deprive that person of meaningful participation in the political process. Americans of the Eighteenth century were very much aware of these uses of both political and economic power, and they were determined to prevent abuses of such power in their new nation.

Protection of both political and economic freedom required freedom of information. As countless generations of despots, kings and dictators have demonstrated, control of information received by the body politic is the key to maintenance of arbitrary power. Once extinguished, freedom of information is in many instances impossible to restore. It was for this reason that the Bill of Rights was added to our Constitution. It is highly significant that the First Amendment, which guarantees freedom of speech, religion and the press, heads the list.

The First Amendment is based on both experience and conviction that the "truth will out" if all are permitted to have their say. This belief accepts the risk of widely publicized errors of fact and interpretation, but at the same time it invites their refutation. The First Amendment challenges the view that there can be only an official "truth" and at the same time places a heavy responsibility on those citizens who enjoy its protection—and those professionals who practice under its mandate. Where freedoms have been lost, failure to accept their corollary responsibilities often has been the cause.

The Bill of Rights also extends its protective mantel to citizen rights in property. The Fifth Amendment forbids the federal government to deprive a person of property without due process of law. Security in property rights is basic to economic, political and personal freedoms. The incentive to work, to accumulate capital, and to enjoy other personal freedoms based on them would be seriously, if not fatally, undermined if the fruits of those labors could be seized by arbitrary exercise of governmental power.

It was in this context that the American newspaper developed; protected first in its right to seek truth regardless of the path down which truth leads; and second—as free private enterprise—motivated to profit by satisfying the needs of its customers. The American free press, thus, became a bulwark of other freedoms while exercising its own.

This chapter explores the economic setting in which American newspapers operate and the interrelationship of economic and political freedoms so critical to newspapers' survival and service to all Americans.

Birth of the American System

In the late Eighteenth century when basic concepts of democracy were seeking expression, mercantilism was the prevailing political/

economic system of the western world. Kings granted monopolies to established business and political leaders, and smothered "little" businessmen, farmers, working people and consumers with a mass of restrictive regulations.[1] Opponents of mercantilism—Adam Smith and others—developed the theoretical framework for a system of private enterprise, competition and free trade. Their revolutionary idea was that the overall social good is enhanced by providing individuals with freedom to improve their economic position in life. Government's role was to function as an impartial umpire, offering only those social services that were not, or could not be, provided by individuals seeking their own ends.

Liberal economists believed that this "free market" system would promote individual freedom, encourage each individual to work productively and at the same time serve collective interests. The free-market theory impressed certain American founding fathers as an essential "democratic" concept. If "free competition" of parties, candidates, ideas and programs for the votes of the people would force government into line with public desires, then businesses competing for customers should also better serve the people.

In the Constitutional Convention and subsequent ratifying conventions, the founding fathers debated vigorously what type of economic system would best serve the new nation. Alexander Hamilton, the Federalists and the commercial interests of that day wanted to limit free enterprise and full democracy. They favored a strong federal government, responsive to *their* interests and ideas, and they championed an economic policy including many traditions of European mercantilism. Hamilton argued that a controlled economy would be the most efficient.

Thomas Jefferson and James Madison opposed Hamilton and sought individual rights and humanitarian values. They believed economic freedom essential to political and personal freedom, and that owner-operated farms and small-scale businesses should be the cornerstones of the economy. Jefferson conceded that economic democracy might not be as productive as a controlled economy, but he argued that if a choice had to be made, freedom was more important than economic efficiency without freedom. The U.S. enterprise economy—based on a combination of Hamilton's and Jefferson's precepts—rapidly became the most efficient economic system in history. And Americans came to enjoy more individual freedom than any people in history.

Jefferson's view that there is a reciprocal relationship between economic freedom and other freedoms has been vindicated by our national experience. Economics are a part of almost everything we do, including job choice, spending, saving and selection of life-style options. Like the individual citizen, a free press needs substantial economic freedom as well as First Amendment protections in order to maintain its independence and to fulfill its responsibilities in a free, pluralistic society.

Our Economic System

Anyone interested in a free press should also be interested in its economics. American newspapers are business enterprises as well as purveyors of information. If they do not meet the test of profitability that all businesses must meet, they cannot continue to perform their informational roles. Since newspaper income, both in terms of advertising sales and customer purchases, is related to size of readership, there is a constant pressure to improve reporting and to satisfy reader demands in new ways. On the expense side of the ledger, there is a constant pressure to modernize, to print more news at lower unit cost, and to keep a newspaper competitive with other sources of information and entertainment.

As a private enterprise, a newspaper—like other businesses—must constantly strive for efficiency while providing readers with information for which they are willing to pay. In countries where newspapers do not function as private enterprises the source of their financial support—most frequently government—can subordinate economic efficiency and objective reporting to other goals. Such a controlled press is not typically devoted to the protection and promotion of individual freedoms—political or economic—in which a free press and a free society have crucial stakes.

It is clear that the American newspaper business is very much a part of the American enterprise system. We usually say that we have a "free" enterprise system. The fact is, of course, that a system completely free of any controls other than market forces would be chaotic: Who would enforce contracts? Who would protect the consumer from fraud, or the businessman from arbitrary allocations of credit or supplies?

Markets must be orderly; constraints must be applied at various levels of economic activity to protect both buyer and seller. Absolute freedom and an orderly economic system are incompatible. Thus, "free enterprise" as we use and understand the term, connotes a system wherein individual investors, workers, savers and consumers (including newspaper readers and advertisers) are free within the broadest permissible limits to make their own choices. These limits vary, but relative to any other country, the United States indeed has free enterprise. Its major characteristics are: *individualism, consumer choice, competition, the profit motive and varying degrees of governmental intervention.*

Individualism

Individual freedom is the essential element of both political democracy and a free-enterprise economy. In a truly democractic society, human freedom and individual self-determination are paramount. This freedom is indivisible. Chip away freedom of religion, education or press and personal freedoms are diminished. The same is true of economic freedom. Free men require free markets with freedom to choose vocations; to acquire goods, services and property; and to enter into legally binding contracts.

If, as in China and the Soviet Union, government owned all industries, it would control newspapers. In the USSR, freedom of speech is highly curtailed. The official newspaper, *Pravda,* includes only those news items the Communist Party wants reported, regardless of their import. In addition, there are very few new "voices." Individuals who dare to speak out against the "establishment" are subject to official criticism and sometimes punished. In the United States, on the other hand, constitutionally-guaranteed free speech and the privately owned free press foster presentation of competing points of view, many of which are critical of business, government and other social institutions.

One of the basic tenets of free enterprise is the individual's right to own property, permitting the majority of society's wealth to be dispersed among individuals rather than monopolized by government. This dispersal is far from equal, and property and income can also be lost. In a free-enterprise system the opportunity for gain carries with it a risk of loss. It is this very characteristic that gives a true free-enterprise system its dynamism. Complacency, acceptance of inefficiency, and poor decisions court disaster. Thus, a newspaper or any other business is encouraged to continually seek new ways of meeting society's needs and desires more effectively and efficiently.

Consumer Choice in a Free Market

In a free market a business must attract buyers who have a choice between a wide variety of goods and competing suppliers. This freedom of choice gives customers a powerful voice in our economic system. For example, the large and powerful Ford Motor Company spent hundreds of millions of dollars manufacturing, promoting and distributing the Edsel car; but consumers said "no." It had to be withdrawn from the marketplace. On the other hand, the Ford Mustang met enthusiastic acceptance. It was consumer evaluations in a free market that handed out these losses and rewards.

The consumer's role in the U.S. economy is so great that some have advocated that the system be called "consumerism." Consumerism as a label tends to overstate consumers' power, but through their collective dollar votes for and against products and services consumers do play a major role in the allocation of resources and the success or failure of businesses—including newspapers. Although imperfect, American consumers' freedom of choice in the marketplace is unprecedented in history.

Competition

Competition—business rivalry for the patronage of consumers—encourages business firms to improve products and develop new ones, keep prices fairly close to costs, and cater to consumers' desires. Although competition is not always as vigorous as it should be, intense and important business rivalry still characterizes the United States. For example, a newspaper usually must compete vigorously with other newspapers, television, radio, magazines, and recreational pursuits. As any circulation manager will tell you, competition for consumers' attention, time and dollars is most vigorous.

In many nations, business competition is weak. As a result, the economy fails to respond to the full range of consumers' interests. Often such economies cater to the wealthy rather than the masses, and prices are high. In the United States, mass production industries seek profit by lowering price to reach as many consumers as possible. As a result, most prices in the United States—relative to per capita income—are the lowest in the world, primarily due to the efficiency of our economic system and to competition for patronage.

The Profit Motive

In a free-market economy, profits are usually financial rewards for risk-taking investment. The profit motive has prompted millions of citizens to develop businesses and to acquire property. Many legendary U.S. businessmen had humble beginnings; some were penniless immigrants. Men of ability, and sometimes guile, they acquired large fortunes in their drive for profit. Andrew Carnegie and John D. Rockefeller fit that mold. Henry Ford and J. C. Penney saw opportunities to serve the American public by combining quality, durability, service, and reasonable price in their products. Each was richly rewarded.

In communities throughout America there are thousands of highly successful entrepreneurs. At the same time, great industrial enterprises, including some newspapers, have failed to meet the test of profitability and have passed from the scene.

Competition and free-market pricing are, from society's point of view, essential to the success of a profit-oriented economy. In essence, the process is as follows:

1. The lure of potential profit induces risk taking and entrepreneurial activity. As a result of these economic ventures, many successful innovations and enterprises are born into the service of society. Often, but far from always, handsome profits are earned as a reward.

2. The handsome profits attract others to the industry. As competition rises, prices are driven down as each rival seeks the patronage of buyers. In the attempt to maintain patronage and profitability, each rival is provided with substantial incentives to improve the product and to operate as efficiently as possible. For example, the first ballpoint pen—which was not very good relative to today's standards—was popular, even though it cost $20. Profits from this innovative venture attracted others to the industry. Intense competition resulted in product improvements and a rapid decline of prices. Today, one can buy a 19-cent ballpoint that is far better than the original pen which sold for 100 times as much. The recent history of transistors, which revolutionized radio and television manufacturing, and of digital watches is similar. Profits attract competition; competition reduces prices and profits and eventually eliminates inefficient or marginal producers. The process does not always work perfectly because of barriers to entry and competition. However, a true free enterprise economy works to eliminate such obstacles.

Profits are indispensable to the success of a private-enterprise system because they are both *the major source of capital accumulations needed for economic progress and the incentive and reward for investing capital.* Capital is essential in all economic systems and profits are the compensation of capital—just as wages and salaries are the compensation of labor. In short, profits are part of the cost of keeping a business going.

While most consumers imagine that profits are far higher than they really are, a few businessmen erroneously believe profits to be the overriding purpose of all private enterprise. These views and the social role of profit will be examined in Chapter 4.

From society's standpoint, the purpose of a business—newspaper or otherwise—is to efficiently provide goods and services satisfying society's needs and desires. In a free-market system, resources are allocated according to the potential rewards to be earned in serving society in various ways.

In a controlled economy, the cost of capital still exists. As management expert, Peter Drucker writes, "If archangels instead of businessmen sat in directors' chairs, they still would have to be concerned with profitability, despite their total lack of personal interest in making profits. This applies with equal force to those far from angelic individuals, the commissioners who run Soviet Russia's business enterprises, who have to run businesses on a higher profit margin than the 'wicked' capitalists of the West."[2] But in this context, "profit" is a measure of performance, not a motivation to enter new and untried fields in response to perceived consumer needs and opportunities for profit.

The concept of profit is integrated into socialistic as well as free market economic systems. For instance, Yugoslavia, a relatively poor nation, is enjoying a rapid rate of economic growth. Many economists attribute Yugoslavia's success to its decentralized economic and political system, with enterprises operated by employe councils on a profit-sharing basis. Personal incentives are not frowned upon. Instead, they are enshrined in the socialist principle "from each according to his abilities—to each according to his labor." Worker-elected councils set pay scales and prices, select executives, make investment decisions and strive to earn a profit.[3] But one must still ask who ultimately controls resources and allocations of capital and to what extent are workers and consumers free to make their own choices.

In summary, a free-enterprise economy relies on individual initiative and on private ownership of productive resources. Consumers play a powerful role in the allocation of those resources because of their freedom in the marketplace. While the prospect of profits provides a major incentive for engaging in economic activity, consumer choice and competition ultimately control who receives profits and in what amount. If abnormally high profits are earned in a given industry, others are attracted to it and competition for consumers' patronage drives prices and profits down. Despite many imperfections, the reality of America's economy approximates this model.

The Role of Government

In a free-enterprise economy, a key role of government is to protect property rights and competition. This role includes protecting consumers and honest businessmen against unscrupulous practices. Also, government seeks to provide for those individuals unable to work or find work, and for defense, police protection and other socially necessary services not normally profitable for private industry. In reality, the United States has departed in many ways from the pure free-enterprise model. For this reason our economic way of life might best be called the "American Enterprise System."

Even the most ardent advocate of the U.S. economic system must concede that it has weaknesses. For example, social discrimination has caused inequities in education, job opportunities and, therefore, income. In a true free-market economy, there is no room for social discrimination in employment or its rewards; each individual is rewarded on the basis of his or her demonstrated ability to contribute to the economy. Since World War II the United States has been moving toward more equal opportunity for all. This progress has required government intervention, not because of a perversity of free enterprise, but because of historic social discrimination contrary to the economic, political and social philosophy of a free society.

Another distortion of the U.S. economy has been the lack of vigorous competition is some industries. Ironically, this lack of business rivalry often has been due to government involvement. For example, the highly regulated transportation industry is frequently cited as lacking competition. Consumer advocate Ralph Nader and Lewis Engman, past chairman of the Federal Trade Commission, have both advocated a return to the rigors of competition to regulate American economic life. As Engman points out, ". . . much of today's regulatory machinery does little more than shelter producers from the normal competitive consequences of lassitude and inefficiency. . . . The consumer, for whatever presumed abuse he is being spared, is paying plenty in the form of government-sanctioned price fixing." Engman uses regulation of trucking rates as an example: ". . . when the Supreme Court held some time ago that fresh dressed poultry was an agricultural commodity under the ICC (Interstate Commerce Commission) Act and thus not subject to regulation, the average rate for shipping it fell by 33 percent."[4]

Free enterprise and free markets will not work if they are only given lip service while businessmen turn to government for protection against the rigors of competition. On the other hand, misinformation about the functioning of the American enterprise system, lack of widespread understanding of its basic principles, and publicity about the wrongdoing of a few have posed challenges to the system. Should the American enterprise system fail, America's free press would be among the first of the victims.

What is at stake is not just economic freedom, but all the liberties to which free newspapers and a free society are so inseparably tied.

Conclusion

American newspapers are private enterprises operating in an essentially free-market economy. They are protected by the Constitution and dependent upon economic independence. Because of the essential role of economic freedom in protection of our other freedoms, one cannot truly understand the American newspaper without viewing it as both a journalistic and a business enterprise.

NOTES
Chapter 1

[1] O. H. Taylor, "Free Enterprise and Democracy," *Saving American Capitalism,* (New York, New York: Alfred A. Knopf, 1948), p. 338. This book, edited by Seymour E. Harris, is a collection of political economy essays by liberal economists.

[2] Peter Drucker, *Management: Tasks, Responsibilities, Practices* (New York, N.Y.: Harper & Row, 1973, 1974), p. 60.

[3] "Yugoslavia's System of Letting Employees Manage Business Works Surprisingly Well," *Wall Street Journal,* October 8, 1975, p. 36.

[4] Lewis A. Engman, Address before the 1974 Fall Conference of the Financial Analysts Federation, Detroit, Michigan.

2

Economic Status of U. S. Newspapers

As ALREADY SUGGESTED, the free press of the United States rests on two foundations:
- The First Amendment, or the right to report the news.
- Economic security, or the means to report the news.

Because economic independence is necessary for preservation of a free press, the growth and strength of the newspaper business should be of interest to all who are concerned with maintaining a free and informed citizenry.

A major purpose of this chapter is to measure and evaluate economic progress of the daily newspaper since World War II. Throughout the analysis, the growth of the newspaper is compared to the growth of all other manufacturing industries and to the U.S. economy.

Social Significance of Newspapers

Newspapers are the major medium for local, national and international news and for editorials, advertising and shopping information. In fact, newspapers are one of the largest industries in the United States, ranking third in number of employes.[1]

While this book is concerned primarily with the economics of America's newspapers, their social significance goes far beyond their economic contribution.

The U.S. newspaper is a unique *social* institution—the product of social demand and of a democratic political and economic system. As the canons of the American Society of Newspaper Editors (ASNE) explicitly acknowledge, a newspaper's duty is to perform in the public interest, however variously that interest is defined.

First, newspapers present information and interpretation of news. *The prime function of a newspaper is to satisfy the public's need to know, that is, to provide "a truthful, comprehensive and intelligent account of the day's events in a context which gives them meaning."* [2] This implies "barebone" news plus in-depth, unbiased reporting which facilitates analysis and interpretation. Without facts and in-depth reporting, an informed public and a viable democracy cannot exist. A newspaper's treatment of a subject or event must be full enough to give meaning to events and to connect facts separated in time and place.

The communications function of a newspaper goes beyond discussion of local, national and international events. According to a Newspaper Advertising Bureau study, more than three-fourths of participating newspapers regularly carried special columns or sections on business and finance, fashion, food and recipes, health and medicine, personal advice and television programs. Between three-fifths and three-quarters carried features on beauty, books, bridge, agriculture, movies, stock quotations, sewing, teenage activities and the theatre.[3] Through these features, newspapers entertain and educate.

For many, newspapers are an economic tool for daily living. Newspaper advertising provides readers with information about the availability and prices of goods and services. People find that they miss advertising when they are without a newspaper.[4] Studies show that buyers of television sets, furniture and small appliances rely heavily on information from advertising.[5]

Newspapers also serve retailers, financial institutions, political candidates, persons seeking jobs, companies offering jobs and thousands of others who advertise each day. Newspapers are the nation's most frequently used advertising medium.

Newspapers also provide comment and criticism. With editorial pages and letters to the editor, newspapers help fight their readers' battles, and provide a forum for public debate. In addition, newspapers frequently act as auditors of government and of society at large, and perform an important role in safeguarding personal liberties: "One great danger we face in our century is the public feeling that events are beyond control, that the individual is powerless to affect the march of history. The newspaper has the unique ability to view with alarm, to create issues and to offer plans for positive action. Thus it offers links between people's individual and private interests and those which they share with the rest of society."[6]

While newspapers do not perform each of their several functions perfectly and without the aid of other media, they are an essential element of our political and economic way of life. Their primary function—the gathering and dissemination of news and information—is indispensable to freedom, democracy and progress. Available at a price almost everyone can afford, newspapers are the nation's largest medium keeping people alert to issues and problems they face each day.

Like any other viable business or institution, the free press requires a healthy economic foundation. This foundation is an absolute necessity for the maintenance of an independent and free press. However, the strength of this foundation is, to a major extent, determined by how well the newspaper has served its various publics.

Number of Newspapers

The number of daily newspapers has held steady since World War II. As in any competitive industry, there have been some closures, particularly in large cities. But, because of the founding of new papers there are about as many dailies today as there were 30 years ago.[7] The number of Sunday newspapers has increased from 497 in 1946 to 650 in 1976—a gain of 31 percent.

Of the 1,762 daily newspapers in 1976, 1,512 were of less than 50,000 circulation, reflecting the population of the towns and cities they served. Some 250 dailies had circulations of more than 50,000.

The fact that there are almost as many daily and more Sunday newspapers today as there were 30 years ago reflects the continuing vitality of the newspaper business. And, of course, there are thousands more less-than-daily newspapers.

With economies of scale in manufacturing and distribution, there normally is a tendency for the largest firms of an industry to grow larger while small ones retire, thus decreasing the total number of firms. As a result, most manufacturing industries have become increasingly concentrated since World War II. The growth pattern of the newspaper business has *not* conformed to this general pattern. In fact, many of the nation's smaller newspapers have achieved their greatest growth during recent decades.

A Major Employer

Newspapers are one of the nation's largest employers. In 1977, an estimated 383,000 Americans worked for newspapers. Among the 451 manufacturing classifications, only steel mills and automobile-parts producers employed more people than newspaper publishers.[8]

That does not include the tens of thousands producing newsprint, printing presses, computers and other products used by our nation's newspapers. It is not possible to determine accurately the number employed by these suppliers of goods and services to newspapers. Many thousands more deliver newspapers but do not work directly for them.

As shown in Figure 1, employment in the newspaper business has increased more rapidly than total employment in the United States. From 1947 through 1976, newspaper employment grew from 248,500 to 381,000, a 53.3 percent gain. Except for slight declines in four years, newspaper employment has risen since World War II.[9]

The 53.3 percent growth of newspaper employment is substantially larger than the 21.9 percent increase of all manufacturing employment and equal to the growth of total U.S. employment. In addition, newspapers are major employers of women, according to the U.S. Department of Labor. In 1976 newspapers employed 124,600 women, an increase of 28 percent since 1970.

Newspaper Income

The economic base of newspapers is provided by the two major publics they serve—advertisers and readers. Total receipts from newspaper publishing reached a record high of $11.2 billion in 1976 and were expected to reach $12.75 billion in 1977.[10]

For all newspapers, including weeklies, revenues from the sale of advertising linage constitute about 65 percent of newspaper income. The remaining 35 percent comes primarily from subscriptions and sales. Specifically, many newspapers derive 25 percent of their income from circulation revenues and approximately 10 percent from auxiliary enterprises such as commercial printing and the sale of syndicated features.[11]

Figure 1

Growth of Employment in the Newspaper Business All Manufacturing Industries and the Total Economy 1947-1976

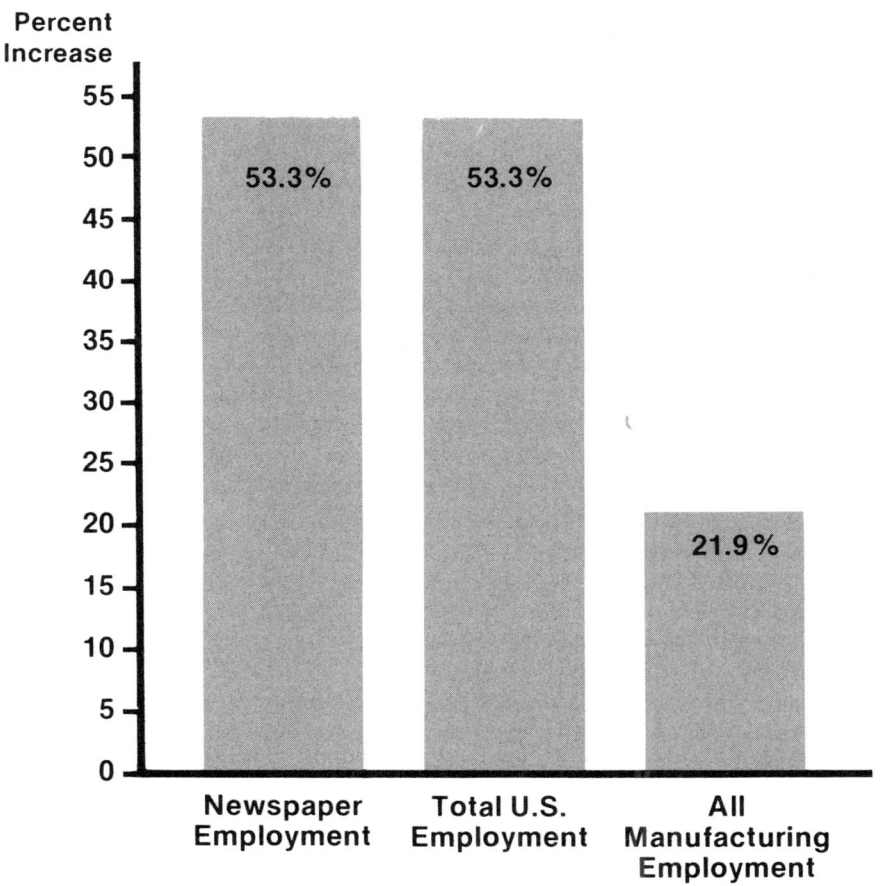

Source: U.S. Department of Labor, Bureau of Labor Statistics.

Newspaper Advertising

Spending for newspaper advertising has grown slightly faster than the U.S. economy, expanding eightfolk since World War II. As shown in Figure 2, newspaper advertising reached $10.2 billion in 1976, 8.8 times that of 1946, whereas the gross national product in 1976 was about 8.1 times larger.

Of the $10.2 billion spent on newspaper advertising in 1976, approximately 85 percent was for local advertising, including classified, and 15 percent for national advertising. National advertising in newspapers rose from less than a quarter billion in 1946 to over $1.5 billion in 1976—a 541 percent increase. Local newspaper advertising increased from $917 million in 1946 to $8.7 billion in 1976—a 847 percent gain. Total spending for newspaper advertising has grown 784 percent since World War II, while the nation's GNP expanded 711 percent.

The expansion of newspaper advertising has benefited both advertisers and the consuming public. Most newspaper advertising is informative, describing in words and pictures what products are available, from whom and at what prices. This information enables consumers to shop and to compare by reading newspaper ads in their homes.

A series of studies at the University of Wisconsin shows that buyers of small appliances, television sets and living room furniture do much of their shopping by reading advertisements, discussing products and brands with friends and relatives and relying on their past experience with retailers and brands.[12] This out-of-store shopping produces a tentative decision to purchase a desired product at a selected store. A trip to that store results in a sale if the consumer's expectations are met. For example, most (73 percent) of the purchases of small electrical appliances were planned prior to shopping in a store. Furthermore, high-income consumers were more likely to make purchase decisions prior to visiting a store—85 percent of those with annual incomes over $15,000 made pre-store buying decisions.

The studies also showed that consumers relied more heavily on newspaper ads than on any other advertising in buying household furniture and television sets. For example fifty-six percent of those buyers used newspaper ads while only 21 percent used magazine advertising; 16 percent, catalogs; 14 percent, television commercials, and 10 percent, radio advertising.

The newspaper also was rated as being the most helpful advertising medium. With such findings, it is not surprising that advertisers have found it profitable to invest more money in newspaper advertising than in any other medium.

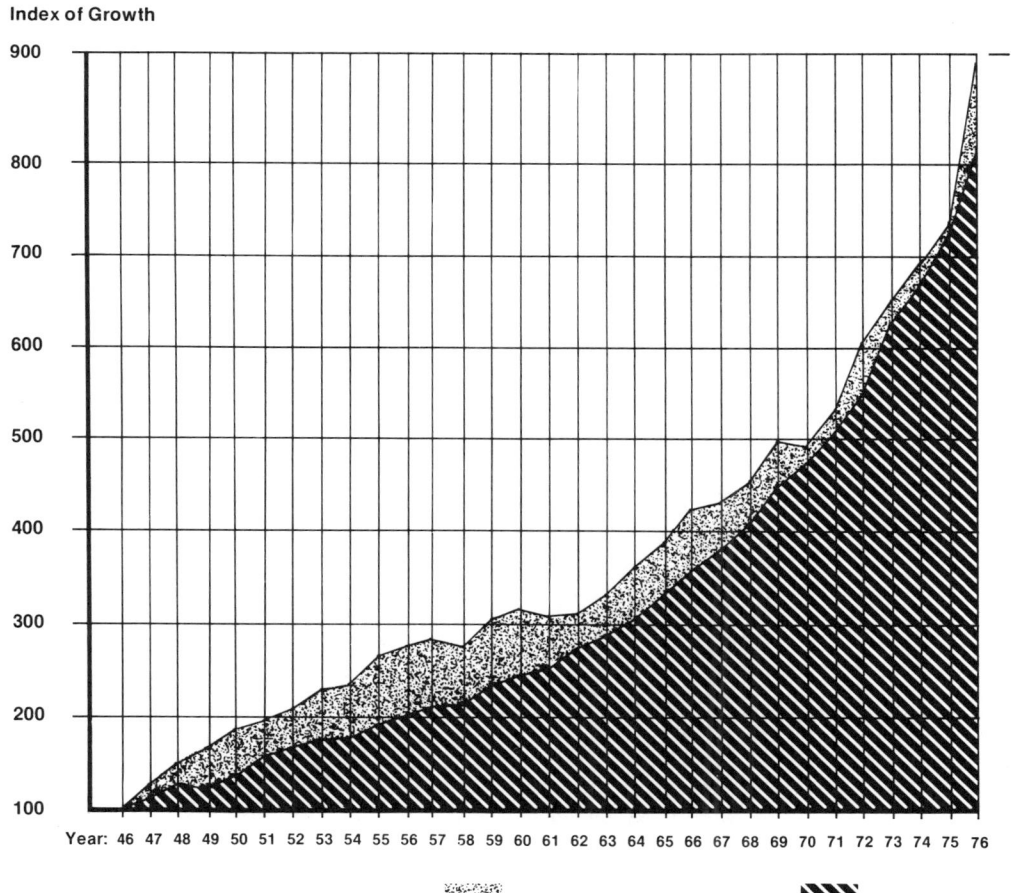

30 □ The Economics of the American Newspaper

As shown in Figure 3, newspapers received 30.0 percent of all 1976 advertising expenditures—more than television and radio combined.

In 1946, newspapers held 34 percent of the advertising market. The introduction and growth of television cut into that share. Still, newspaper advertising has grown faster than the economy and newspapers continue to be the largest advertising medium. And, in recent years, the newspaper share of total advertising dollars has risen. As of 1963 newspaper's share was at a post-World War II low of 29 percent; more recently, it has fluctuated around 30 percent. As pointed out by the U.S. Department of Commerce, "Newspaper advertising revenue today is almost as great as television, radio, and magazine advertising revenue combined."[13] In fact, the *growth* of newspaper advertising since World

Figure 3

Shares of Total Advertising By Major Media—1976

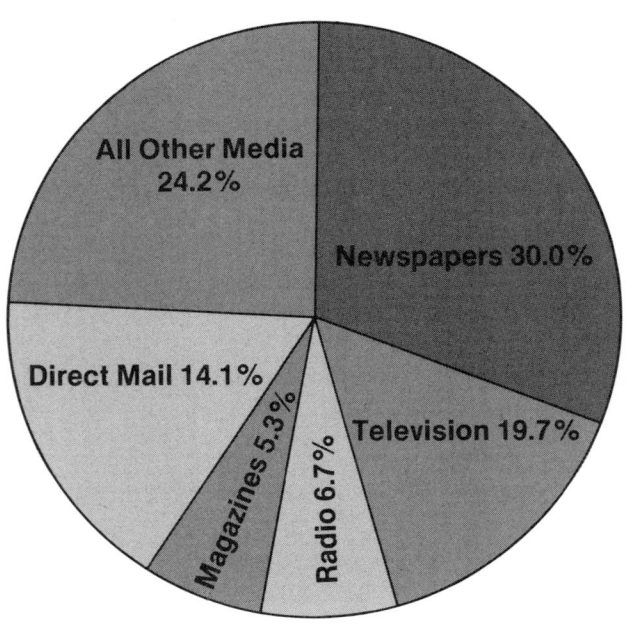

Source: McCann Erickson, Inc., Newspaper Advertising Bureau

War II exceeds by 38 percent the volume of television advertising today.

Circulation

The daily circulation of U. S. newspapers approached 61 million in 1976, compared with less than 51 million in 1946. Daily circulation has risen 20 percent since 1946 while total U.S. population has increased over 50 percent. This is not a very useful comparison because babies and small children do not buy and read newspapers; older children and some young adults are not frequent newspaper buyers because they rely on the family newspaper or that of the dormitory or other living unit; elderly persons, living with relatives or in institutions, often read newspapers purchased by others. As shown in Figure 4, there was, until 1967, a close parallel between increases in daily circulation and increases in the population between the ages of 21 and 65. However, since 1967 daily circulation has not kept pace with the growth of the adult population.

Several sociological and economic factors are involved:

- Historically, a substantial proportion of the population read more than one newspaper a day. As newspapers have grown larger and more comprehensive, fewer consumers find time to read two or more each day.

- Since World War II, the established media have had to make room for television, which fills time formerly devoted to a second or third newspaper.

- Thanks to a rising standard of living, boating, golfing, camping and other recreational activities now occupy a larger proportion of our leisure time.

- Inner-city deterioration and a "flight" to suburban areas have reduced newspaper readership in some large cities. First, urban crime has decreased pedestrian traffic in downtown areas after dark, reducing newspaper sales. Poor conditions in core-city areas have reduced home deliveries in these markets. And, apartment house dwellers often are harder for newspapers to serve than people living in single-family homes.

- The move to the suburbs has created communities not served by buses or trains. Industry dispersal to the suburbs also has decreased the ability of public transportation to serve an increasingly scattered population. A person driving to work cannot read a newspaper, but a train or bus commuter can.

- The dramatic growth of daily small-city and town newspapers, with their improved coverage of national and international events, has reduced out-of-town circulation of metropolitan newspapers. In many the population in that age bracket will expand substantially in the years ahead.

Newspaper Versus National Growth

Newspaper publishing is a well-established business. In fact, it is one of the oldest lines of business enterprise, preceding the birth of our nation by well over 200 years.[14] Mature industries usually expand more slowly than the total economy, because they have long passed their growth stage and the total economy includes many newly developing industries as technology and the standard of living increases. However, U.S. newspapers have had a remarkable growth record since World War II.

The most significant measure of real newspaper growth is newsprint consumption. Consumption of the paper on which newspapers are printed reflects changes in advertising volume, editorial content and circulation. While newspapers are the primary consumers of newsprint, telephone directories, shoppers and catalogs also are printed on newsprint. For many years, daily newspapers reporting to the American Newspaper Publishers Association accounted for about 86 percent of the nation's total consumption. That ratio fell to 80 percent in 1976, reflecting a rapid growth in preprinted advertising inserts.

Newsprint used for preprinted advertising inserts is not included in the consumption data of newspapers. However, preprinted advertising, which substitutes for traditional advertising, is very much a part of the daily newspaper.[15] The use of "preprints" is a relatively recent development, and therefore causes newsprint consumption statistics to understate newspapers' true growth during the last decade.

The newsprint consumption of daily newspapers declined during 1974 and 1975 because of paper conservation measures adopted by publishers and a severe national recession. The conservation measures were prompted by a rapid escalation of newsprint prices.[16]

As shown in Figure 5, newsprint consumption increased from 4.3 million tons in 1946 to over 10.6 million in 1974, a 147 percent growth.[17] Without increased efficiency in newsprint use, consumption probably would have exceeded 11.1 million tons—a post-World War II growth of 158 percent. As these statistics indicate, newspaper growth has greatly exceeded U.S. population growth.

The combination of nationwide recession and inflation did severely hurt the newspaper business in 1975. Advertising linage declined, the newshole (editorial content) was reduced in many newspapers and the number of U.S. daily newspapers decreased by eight. This, combined

Figure 5

Newspaper Growth as Measured by Changes in Newsprint Consumption 1946-1976[1]

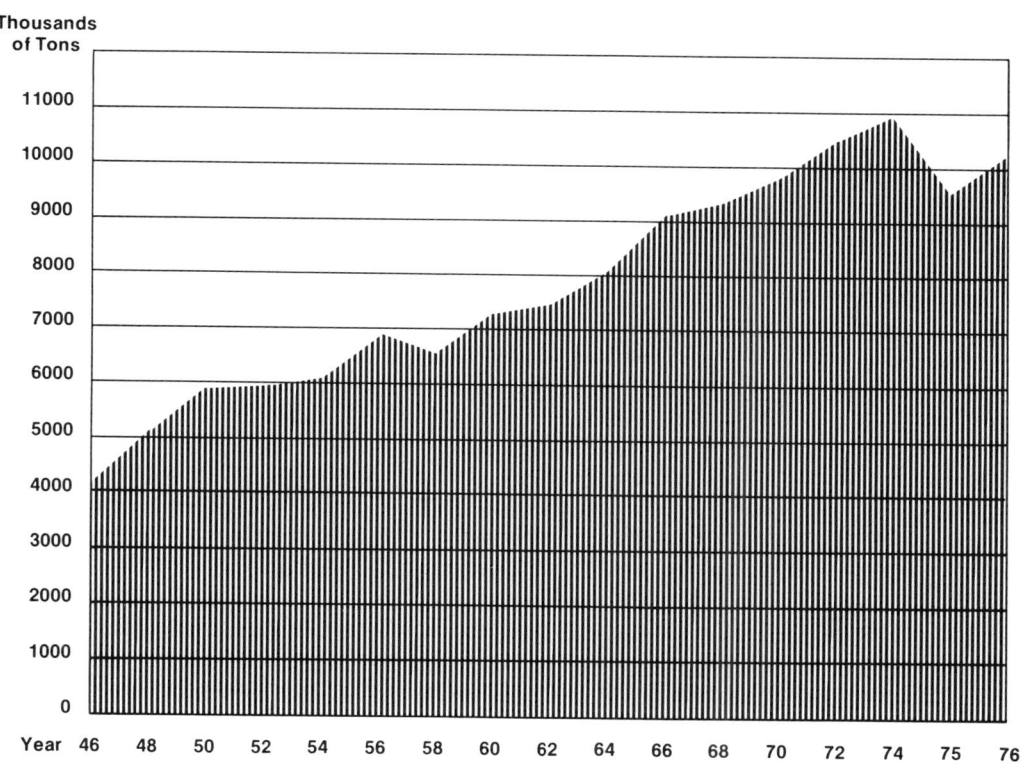

[1]32-pound basis weight newsprint.

Source: ANPA

with the "conservation" of an estimated 570,000 tons of newsprint by all users caused newsprint consumption to decline to an adjusted total of 10.2 million tons. (Reported tonnage was actually 9.1 million tons, but because of the reduction in the average weight of newsprint used, that figure was adjusted upward to permit comparisons with past decades.) With economic recovery in 1976, newspaper growth resumed and newsprint consumption rose 5 percent. However, the growth rate accelerated to about 10 percent in 1977.

Figure 6

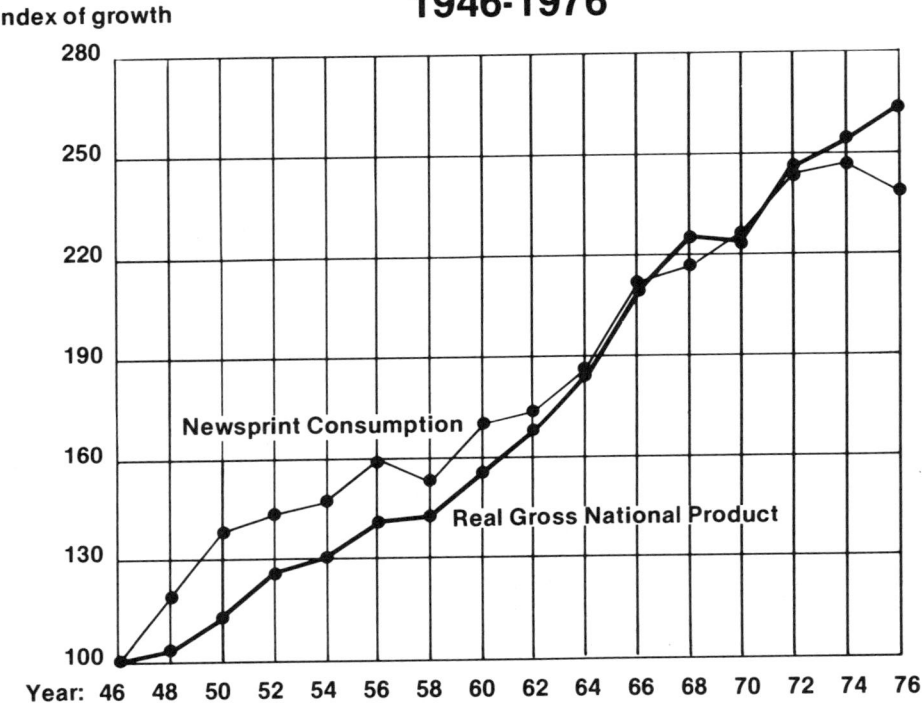

Source: ANPA; U.S. Department of Commerce

While newspaper growth can be measured in terms of newsprint consumption, the best measure of overall economic growth is the real gross national product. Gross national product in constant dollars (minus inflation) reflects both the population increase and the nation's rising standard of living. As shown in Figure 6, the growth of the newspaper business has tended to parallel the general growth of the economy. Real gross national product grew 165 percent during the 1946–1976 period. Newsprint consumption expanded 140 percent during the same period—153 percent when adjusted for conservation measures.

A Recent Decade

In recent decades, newspaper growth has varied by geographical region. For example, in the 1965–1975 period daily newspapers in the South enjoyed the highest growth rate as measured by newsprint consumption. Their usage of paper rose 27 percent during the decade, as shown in Table 1.

Table 1

INCREASES IN NEWSPRINT CONSUMPTION BY U.S. DAILY NEWSPAPERS IN VARIOUS GEOGRAPHIC REGIONS 1965–1975 [1]

Region	1965 Consumption	1975 Consumption	1965–1975 Tons	Percent Change
Northeast	2,031,263	1,951,818	−79,445	− 3.9
North Central	1,969,655	1,964,128	−5,527	− 0.3
South	1,646,910	2,082,747	435,837	26.5
West	1,301,760	1,370,759	68,999	5.3
Total	6,949,588	7,369,452	419,864	6.0
Total U.S. Consumption by All Users	8,143,396	9,150,165	1,006,769	12.4

Source: Daily newspapers reporting to ANPA.

[1] The data do not include foreign language newspapers, college newspapers, special service dailies, The Christian Science Monitor, The Wall Street Journal, The Journal of Commerce and The Daily Racing Form. Consumption data are adjusted for temporary losses due to major strikes against newspapers. The 1965 data are adjusted to the average basis weight of 1975. Both 1965 and 1975 data are adjusted for the effect of strikes against newspapers.

Newsprint consumption of northeastern dailies decreased by 4 percent, reflecting relatively slow growth of the economy and population in that region, and the demise of several metropolitan newspapers.

Expansion of daily newspapers has also varied substantially by city size. Dailies in towns and cities of less than 100,000 population, as shown in Table 2, expanded 31 percent during the decade 1965–1975.

The next highest growth rate occurred in cities of 100,000 to 250,000 population—their newsprint consumption grew 15 percent.

On the other end of the spectrum, newspapers in the largest cities with one million or more population consumed 8.3 percent less newsprint in 1975 than in 1965.

Table 2
INCREASES IN NEWSPRINT CONSUMPTION BY U.S. DAILY NEWSPAPERS IN CITIES OF VARIOUS SIZES 1965–1975[1]

City Size	1965		1975		1965–1975 Tons	Percent Change
	No. of Newspapers	Consumption	No. of Newspapers	Consumption		
Less than 100,000	1,498	1,430,619	1,507	1,876,489	445,870	31.2
100,000 to 250,000	117	802,057	116	923,816	121,759	15.2
250,000 to 500,000	61	1,110,162	59	1,174,316	64,154	5.8
500,000 to 1 million	47	1,601,050	45	1,555,044	− 46,006	− 2.9
1 million and over	20	2,005,700	17	1,839,787	−165,913	− 8.3
All Daily Newspapers	1,743	6,949,588	1,744	7,369,452	419,864	6.0

Source: Daily newspapers reporting to ANPA.
[1] See footnote 1, Table 1.

Conclusion

The newspaper business, only one part of the communications industry, is one of the largest businesses in the United States. Although newspapers are an "old business," they have exhibited great strength and vitality over the past few decades. They have successfully adjusted to a rapidly changing society, the introduction of television and a change in reading habits. The growth of newspapers has about equalled the growth of the economy. Expenditures on newspaper advertising have grown more rapidly than the gross national product. Newspaper employment has expanded faster than U.S. manufacturing employment. Newsprint consumption has increased nearly as rapidly as the "real" gross national product. However, circulation growth has lagged the expansion of population.

There is little doubt that newspapers will expand in the years ahead. (The immediate future will be examined in Chapter 10.) Newspapers will continue to be the nation's largest medium for news and advertising. The future growth of newspapers should continue to provide the economic independence necessary for preservation of a free press in a democratic society.

NOTES
Chapter 2

[1] U. S. Department of Commerce—Domestic and International Business Administration, *U. S. Industrial Outlook 1977*, p. 348.

[2] *A Free and Responsible Press,* The Report of the Commission on Freedom of the Press (Chicago: University of Chicago Press, 1947), pp. 20–21.

[3] Leo Bogart, "Changing News Interests and the News Media," *Public Opinion Quarterly,* Vol. 32, No. 4 (Winter 1968–1969), p. 569.

[4] J. Edward Gerald, *The Social Responsibility of the Press* (Minneapolis: University of Minnesota Press, 1963), p. 110.

[5] Bruce LeGrande and Jon G. Udell, "Consumer Behavior in the Market Place: An Empirical Study in the Television and Furniture Fields with Theoretical Implications," *Journal of Retailing,* Vol. 40, No. 3 (Fall 1964), pp. 32–41, and Jon G. Udell, "Prepurchase Behavior of Buyers of Small Electrical Appliances," *Journal of Marketing,* Vol. 30, No. 4 (October 1966), pp. 50–52.

[6] Bogart, *Op.Cit.,* p. 570.

[7] In 1946 there were 1,763 daily newspapers in the United States; as of 1976 there were 1,762 dailies.

[8] U. S. Department of Commerce, *Op. Cit.,* p. 349. The Commerce Department classifies newspapers manufacturers.

[9] *Ibid.*

[10] *Ibid.*

[11] A more detailed picture of newspaper revenues is presented in Chapter 7.

[12] LeGrande and Udell, *Op. Cit.*

[13] U.S. Department of Commerce—Business and Defense Services Administration, *U.S. Industrial Outlook* (December, 1969), p. 61.

[14] Newspapers originated in Europe after the invention of moveable type in the fifteenth century.

[15] For a more detailed description of "preprints," see Chapter 7, p. 111.

[16] Newsprint conservation measures include the reduction of trim, smaller white margins, fewer breaks and tears, better use of roll ends, improved storage and handling with less damage to rolls, reduced press overruns, and elimination of marginal circulations. The ANPA has estimated that conservation measures during just the last two years have saved 570,000 tons of newsprint. For a more detailed discussion of newsprint prices, see Chapter 8, pp. 124–125.

[17] Actual tonnage consumed in 1974 was 10.2 million tons. However, the weight of newsprint has been reduced by most suppliers. When adjusted for this change, the 10.6 million-ton figure is obtained. In early 1977, the estimation procedures for determining newsprint consumption were changed. All of the above data are based upon the historically used procedures because revisions for years preceding 1966 are not available.

3

The Marketing Concept and Newspaper Organization

THE PRIMARY SOCIAL and economic purpose of a business is to serve its customers and society well and with maximum efficiency. Efficiency depends on many factors, including marketing and organizational concepts and skills.

Marketing and the Marketing Concept

According to a traditional but obsolete view, marketing is the distribution and sale of goods; marketing was seen as a final operation—what happens between the last station on an assembly line and the ultimate sale of the product to a customer. In this sense, newspapers have been marketing for as long as they have existed.

The modern view encompasses a broader "marketing concept" that begins with determination of customer needs. According to this view, marketing is the combination of product planning, pricing, promotion, distribution and service—all designed to fulfill customers' needs.[1]

The phrase "customers' needs" suggests a philosophy as well as a common goal for all the activities of a newspaper. Both the social service and the profitability of any business venture are, to a major extent, determined by how well the customer is served.

Marketing was refined to a high degree by many businesses after World War II and many individual marketing techniques were adopted in piecemeal fashion by newspapers. But while other producers package products such as cosmetics or cereals, a newspaper packages what its professional editors perceive to be objective and relevant facts about the world. Also, newspapers are involved in marketing in another, quite different way: they are a paid marketing vehicle for those who use newspapers to transmit advertising messages for goods and services to potential customers.

Challenge of the Press

The professional challenge of the free press is how to present *objective* facts and news about the world and sometimes *subjective* promotion for an advertised product and still retain believability and respect from its readers. Can a newspaper's business self-interest—its need to attract and hold advertising—be allowed to modify its primary news mission?

In 1911 a group of Chicago newspapermen felt so keenly that the press should be absolutely uncompromised by any dependence upon advertising that they launched an adless newspaper, the *Chicago Day Book*. One of its moving spirits was poet and historian Carl Sandburg. The paper, a penny daily published in a 7-by-10 inch format, died in 1917.

In 1940, another adless newspaper, the New York City daily *PM*, was founded. The editors and writers of *PM* operated with complete freedom from the influence of any outside source. It expired in 1948.

Neither experiment provided an enduring answer to the problem of news independence from advertisers and advertising. But many editors long ago developed a pragmatic solution: Make every effort to keep advertising and puffery out of news columns, and keep the paper's ad salesmen out of the newsroom.

Most newspapers followed this rule. The news side covered the day's news as it developed. The ad side sold ads; production people printed the paper; circulators sold it—all in a sequence of largely independent operations.

Although the separation eased ethical problems, it made adoption of the marketing concept difficult, since an essential element of that concept is a company-wide, *unified* effort to meet customers' needs and to earn a profit. The isolation and autonomy of various newspaper departments—even for the highest of motives—raised barriers against the kind of unified effort required by the marketing concept. Therefore, more and more newspapers are moving gradually toward limited market-oriented operations *without sacrificing editorial objectivity.*

Newspapers Serve Two Markets

The marketing concept suggests first finding out what people need and will buy and then providing it. It is not simple to forecast future needs and buying behavior, even by a single, clearly defined customer group. Many large and famous firms, with the best research and marketing minds, often fail in this kind of prediction.[2]

The complications are compounded for newspapers because they serve two customer categories—readers and advertisers. In addition, each is fragmented into many subcategories, each looking to the newspaper for satisfaction of a different need.

How Editors Try to Determine Reader Interests

Editors try to learn what readers want by asking them. Occasionally in smaller markets, questionnaires are inserted into home-delivered copies for readers to rank newspaper features and suggest what they want added or emphasized. Editors also confer with solicitors who go from door to door selling subscriptions. Such sessions enlighten both editors and solicitors and help both better sell their paper.

Reader complaints shape editorial decisions—as when a comic strip is dropped or when the newspaper covers a topic felt by some readers to be inappropriate in a family newspaper. In addition, editors' business and social contacts produce endless suggestions for changes in the content or emphasis of their newspapers.

But, all of the foregoing may not comprise a true cross-section of the market. Additional techniques have been developed in an effort to obtain more representative and reliable information. One such technique is the readership study. Researchers visit with readers chosen in accordance with acceptable statistical sampling procedures and ask what they happened to see or read in a particular newspaper issue. Such studies indicate what items interest most readers. They also provide insight into editorial techniques and content mixes that enhance readership. However, the ranking of content does not necessarily indicate the intensity of reader feeling concerning it. To the bridge buff or crossword addict, the bridge column or crossword puzzle may be the main reason he or she buys the paper.

Other studies include those based on "encounter groups," in which small groups of a half dozen or so readers are encouraged to volunteer their opinions in a free-for-all discussion of the newspaper. There are also "associative studies" designed to reveal whether a paper is perceived to be more for a rich or a poor person; more for an educated person; more for a Republican than a Democrat, and so on.

Reader studies underscore the fragmented nature of the newspaper audience. Many readers say they need and buy a newspaper for "the news"; others for a columnist, comic, syndicated feature, sports result, market report or food or fashion feature.

Many buy it for a combination of these things, or for its political point of view, reliability or fairness. Others prefer a given newspaper because of its stress on local news or the amount and kind of advertising it carries. Some pick a newspaper by its pleasing makeup.

In good times and bad, many want it for its cents-back grocery coupons, which in large metropolitan dailies often total $20 worth in a single issue.

A newspaper is many things to many people. And those things change as our dynamic society evolves.

How Circulators Try to Determine What Readers Want

Newspaper circulation departments are particularly concerned with the reader as a customer, since their job is to sell and deliver the joint product of the news and advertising departments. Their operations fall into two main marketing categories—home-delivery subscriptions and newsstand sales. The first is centered around the sale of subscriptions and delivery of newspapers to subscribers' homes by carrier or by mail.

Home-delivery customers: In a major market, as many as several hundred thousand households receive daily home delivery, a gigantic task involving complex logistics and hundreds of delivery persons. By studying new subscriptions and cancellations—called "starts" and "stops"—circulators keep their fingers on the pulse of subscriber requirements.

Home subscribers demand delivery the same time every day, on the doorstep and not on the porch roof or in the bushes, and they expect a dry paper in rainy or snowy weather. Newspapers and news agencies operate continuous carrier recruitment, training and monitoring programs. Prizes are awarded to carriers for complaint-free service.

Development of home-delivery circulation is costly. Some programs involve the delivery—for days or weeks—of free sample copies to prospective subscribers. The newspaper absorbs the cost of these copies and pays carriers to deliver them. Other programs offer premiums to new subscribers, or prizes to carriers for obtaining new subscriptions, or both. Carrier prizes range in value from a few dollars to trips to Hawaii or Switzerland.

Maintenance of home-delivery circulation is costly because so many people move. Between 1970 and 1974 more than one out of three individuals, 20 years and older, changed addresses. Three of five in the 20–29 age range moved during the same period.[3] As a result, newspapers have to replace or relocate much of their home-delivery circulation every year just to stay even.

Hundreds of thousands of dollars are spent annually by a large newspaper to attract new subscribers. The success or failure of this single activity is a major factor in the profit or loss of a newspaper, and is a major determinant of its continuing utility as an advertising vehicle.

One reason home-delivered circulation is attractive to newspapers in spite of its high cost is that it helps stabilize circulation and revenue. When a newspaper prints a copy destined for a home-delivery reader, it has a sure customer who often has prepaid for his or her newspaper.

The alternative is printing copies to be sold at newsstands or other outlets.

Newsstand customers: Handling the sale of single copies at newsstands and other outlets is the second marketing responsibility of a circulation department. Many single-copy sales are impulse purchases, sparked by the physical presence of the newspaper. Some people will buy a paper if it happens to be convenient, but they will not go out of their way to find one for sale. Therefore, inclement weather or reduced pedestrian traffic decreases "street sales."

When metropolitan newspaper circulators wish to stimulate circulation, they see to it that the maximum number of newsstands are supplied with copies throughout the day's selling cycle. They also place newspaper vending machines and honor boxes at strategic locations not having newsstands.

Keeping all newsstands continuously supplied increases the probability of "returns"—unsold copies which will have no value the next day except as recyclable newsprint. The placement of additional vending machines requires not only their purchase and maintenance, but also additional manpower to keep them supplied and to handle collections.

Content and timing affects newspaper sales. Some customers refuse to buy any edition except the one with the day's final stock quotations. Others will buy only the edition carrying the latest sports news.

Additional single-copy sales occur as the result of another kind of specialized content—news or feature stories involving particular neighborhoods or groups. Astute circulators keep up with the development of such stories, and always make sure that copies are plentifully supplied to newsstands throughout the area figuring in the story.

Advertising, the Second Newspaper Market

There are three main categories of newspaper advertisers—national, retail and classified. Although details of their operations vary, all advertisers have a universal need to move goods or services quickly at the lowest possible ratio of advertising cost to sales.

It is impossible to tell in advance precisely how well any medium will produce sales for an advertiser on a given occasion because there are too many variables beyond control of the medium—including timing, pricing, weather, competition and the economic climate. A newspaper's potential to generate customer response depends mostly on the size and character of its readership. Over the years, advertisers have requested increasingly detailed readership information in an attempt to predict response more accurately.

Decades ago, market population was the major determinant of media decisions for many regional or national advertisers: The larger the population, the more potential customers. Many national advertising budgets were planned on that basis. Similarly, the largest-circulation newspaper was thought to reach most prospects in a market area.

This led to inflated circulation claims and circulation wars. In the days of penny newspapers, one enterprising editor randomly tucked dollar bills into a few hundred copies of his newspaper and advertised that fact on the front page. People rioted at the newsstands to buy multiple copies, which they ripped apart in search of dollar bills and then discarded.

In those days, a claimed circulation of 50,000 might mean a print order of only 5,000, of which only a tiny fraction represented paid copies. One contemporary publisher called that era's circulation figures "as accurate as the Kansas scale"—a rail balanced over a fence.

Such circulation estimates were of no value to advertisers. At their demand, responsible publishers joined advertisers and advertising agents in establishing the Audit Bureau of Circulation in 1914 to conduct independent audits of circulation figures and to monitor circulation procurement methods.[4]

Newspaper advertisers in every category also wanted—and still do—a concentration of circulation near their places of business. Accordingly, newspaper circulation is reported by the average net paid number of copies sold in each of three standard areas or combinations thereof. These are the "city zone," the surrounding "retail trading zone" and "all other." Combined, these constitute the total circulation of a newspaper. Newspapers may also report their circulation to advertisers in other ways to meet their marketing needs, such as circulation within the "standard metropolitan statistical area" or within the "primary marketing area," a multicounty coverage measurement.

As marketing became sophisticated, advertisers wanted information not only on how many copies are sold, but on what kinds of people buy them. This led to coverage and duplication studies which measure the audience of a newspaper according to various demographic criteria, such as sex, age, income, occupation and family size.

Simultaneously, surveys listed which brands were on hand in kitchens, bathrooms and pantries in representative homes, and where the most recent purchases of a wide variety of clothing, home furnishings and other items were made. In some studies data also were gathered on future purchase intentions, vacation plans and business travel.

Such studies usually are made only in large, multinewspaper markets. Where available they are used by retail and national advertisers as a basis for placing newspaper advertising. The studies originally were conducted by individual newspapers or groups using varying methods, sample sizes and questionnaires. Their information could not be consolidated reliably, nor was it helpful to advertisers seeking information on optimum mixtures of different advertising media.

In the early 1960s a new marketing tool was unveiled: the computer. Many executives at first believed the machine would automatically and quickly produce accurate answers to marketing and advertising problems. The early computer's limitation was a lack of information to feed into it, recognized with the wry acronym GIGO—"Garbage In, Garbage Out." To overcome this limitation some newspapers and syndicated research services worked during the 1960s on development of basic multimedia information to feed the computer.

At the same time marketers sought more accurate ways to pin down the key characteristics of consumers of particular products. One of the new developments was the discovery that products with a high rate of consumption and replacement share a common characteristic: A small percentage of users tend to account for a disproportionately large volume of consumption. It was evident that the relatively small number of so-called heavy users in each such commodity category were a primary marketing target, and a brand favored by the heavy users could swiftly achieve market dominance.

New research was launched to identify and profile product users nationwide according to light, medium and heavy usage, demographic characteristics and "penetration" of each group by individual media and by various media in different combinations.

The same information has been gathered for some major, local newspaper markets. When it is fed into a computer, along with the advertising rates for the various media, advertisers can determine which of a variety of alternate media mixes is best to "reach" the desired heavy user or expectant buyer target group in that market. It also is possible to determine whether a particular market, because of some local characteristic, is above or below the national norm in consumption of a particular commodity.

Newspaper advertising market-measuring techniques have come a long way and have become a lot more complicated in a relatively short time; all to point out areas of greatest *potential* consumer response at the lowest cost. But even modern techniques cannot guarantee a precise return. All the variables of timing, pricing, weather, competition and economic climate still are operative.

State of Newspaper Marketing Today

The marketing activities of most newspapers have been fragmented. Different research and marketing techniques have been used by different departments, always in an attempt to find the most practical and quickest way to meet the needs of the department involved. Because of arms'-length interdepartmental relationships, many newspapers apparently have not fully discovered or exploited areas of *mutual* need in their approach to problems.

However, more and more newspapers are moving away from traditional departmental isolationism toward a unified "marketing" approach to all the various missions of the newspaper. In some organizations this appears to have evolved through the kind of happy accident that takes place when cooperative, intuitive people become an effective team; in others, it has come about through conscious effort. The outlook is for still more newspapers to travel the latter route.

Newspaper Organization and the Marketing Concept

The marketing concept is more than it seems. It is a philosophy of management emphasizing that the purpose of a business is to serve consumers, and that profits are earned by serving customers well.

To implement the marketing concept, a newspaper must develop an organizational structure which fosters an integrated response to such questions as:

> What customer need are we meeting? Is it the same need as last year? How do we know? Are we redirecting our efforts to meet changing needs?
> What is the purpose of a given activity?
> How does it relate to other functions of the organization?
> What is the function of the organization itself in the market and as a responsible part of society?
> How might its internal and external relationships be adjusted to make it more effective as a business enterprise and as a social instrument?[5]

These are not just philosophical questions. They are basic and intensely practical. At present, many newspapers are structured in a way that tends to frustrate such questioning and to inhibit application of the marketing concept.

A newspapers' structure is a result of a combination of circumstances. One is the intense pace of newspaper work and the pressure to meet today's deadlines. This typically leads to informal planning, autonomous decisions and prejudice against long-term thinking even at management levels. Another is the complexity of producing a newspaper. Over the past century, the newspaper borrowed much of its thinking and technology from other manufacturing operations. Successful newspapers were those that applied mass production techniques by training employes to perform specialized tasks. With this came compartmentalization and, in many cases, a great dedication to one's specialty than to the whole newspaper. Finally, there is the fundamental belief that democracy requires a free press, independent of internal as well as external forces. Thus the editorial department traditionally is off limits—and should be—for the kind of influence over quality or content that a marketing department might exert over the manufacturing of some other consumer product.

As a result of these factors, the typical newspaper has been structured like a pyramid.

As Figure 1—a greatly simplified diagram—indicates, the editor, advertising manager and circulation manager all report to the publisher, and each is supported by a team of specialists to help him fulfill his mission. Unfortunately, nothing pictured in the diagram relates the newspaper to the customer or to the outside world.

The pyramidal organization is typical not only of many newspapers, but of most universities, government entities, churches and corporations. It breaks the unmanageable whole into manageable parts. It establishes lines of authority and a chain of command.

But the pyramidal approach has a structural drawback which only now is being fully recognized: The newspaper pyramid is made up of smaller pyramids, each with its own specialized, autonomous leader and its own mission. Each leader typically is rewarded for the independent completion of his or her department's mission, without regard to the success or failure of other departments. In some instances this leads to costly, self-canceling efforts by two or more departments.

In some newspapers, each department head acts as though he or she were operating an independent business. The manager is entitled to think so. Little in the organizational scheme suggests that the editor, ad manager or circulation manager has any lateral obligation within the company.

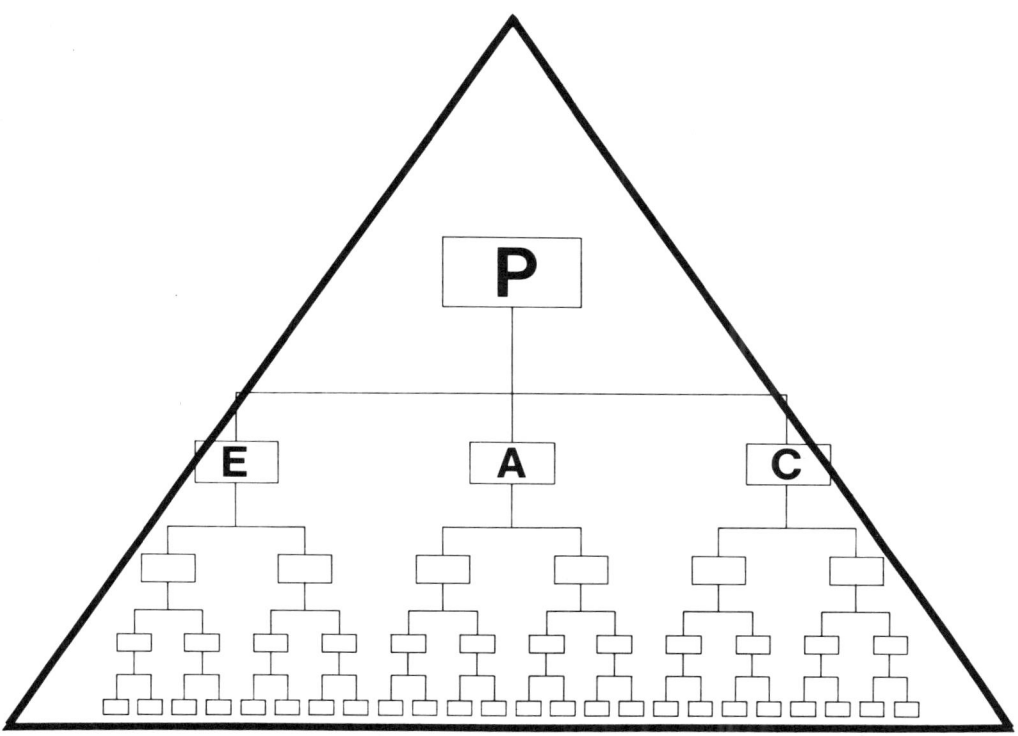

Figure 1
TYPICAL NEWSPAPER STRUCTURE

P-Publisher, E-Editorial Dept., A-Advertising Dept., C-Circulation Dept.

An individual who goes to work in any of the line departments—editorial, production, advertising or circulation—tends to concentrate on that department's mission to the exclusion of other concerns. In most instances, promotion is upward within the same department. A reporter seldom transfers to a supervisory job in advertising. An ad salesperson rarely moves to a job as a home-delivery branch manager.

Even more important, communication and rapport among departments often are impaired. The publisher of one of the nation's largest newspapers was quoted as blaming his paper's economic problems on its hierarchal structure, which divided the paper into what he called "separate fiefdoms dominated by strong men."

A former executive director of the American Press Institute, familiar with every phase of the newspaper business through the seminars conducted by that organization, recently declared that "walls between newspaper departments" create some of the most serious problems facing newspapers today.

The chief executive officer of a major newspaper chain, himself a former editor, was impelled to issue a bulletin forbidding feuding among the department heads of the various newspapers in his group.[6]

A writer on a Midwestern newspaper complained of the hauteur, exclusivity and supercilious attitude of its news reporters, directed not only at the "lesser mortals" in other departments, but also against the paper's feature writers.[7]

Poor cooperation among the retail, national and classified advertising staffs can also be found. One retail ad salesman, when calling on an advertiser to pick up retail copy, recently refused to accept classified copy from the same advertiser for delivery to his own newspaper.[8]

Experts now are developing a new organizational structure for the newspaper that:

—encourages a clearer vision of the contribution of each department and individual to the total effort;
—is uniformly oriented to the customer, to the market and to the social role of the newspaper;
—preserves the freedom of the editorial department to cover the news as it sees fit;
—enables the newspaper to better anticipate and respond to change;
—enhances communication and harmony within the newspaper organization.

Where the Newspaper Functions

A newspaper functions *within and as a reciprocal part of its geographic market.* Understanding this fact and using it as the basis of planning is essential to full realization of a newspaper's potential, and to the success of those who work for it.

The number and kinds of people comprising a market define its size and quality. Their presence generates retail activity. Demographic characteristics—age, sex, income, education, occupation, family size and others—dictate the kind and amount of retail activity the market will support.

The newspaper is totally dependent upon the presence of people, money and retail activity. Newspapers are affected immediately by changes in the market.

A striking example occurred in the 1960s. A Southeastern boom town sprang out of nowhere into bustling prosperity as a major center of the U.S. space exploration program. It attracted thousands of young engineers, technicians, workers and their families. Land developers and retailers rushed to the area to provide housing, goods and services.

The community flourished and grew, and the local newspaper grew along with it. Then the space program was cut back. Overnight, jobs at the space center vanished. Homes were vacated by the hundreds as former space workers left to seek employment elsewhere. Vacated housing was soon taken over—but by retirees.

The population was quickly restored but the town became a different kind of market based on smaller incomes, an older population, lower per-household expenditures and nonexpanding family needs. The difference was reflected in the quantity and kinds of retailers who survived and that, in turn, in the amount and kind of advertising available to the newspaper. This led to a very different newspaper, geared to a very different market.

Ordinarily changes in a market do not occur so quickly and with such dramatic impact. However, *every newspaper's market is changing.* Demographics are in a constant state of flux. For example, Cleveland was the tenth largest city in the United States in 1970. Only three years later it was fifteenth. Similarly, many other large cities of the East and Midwest are losing population while Southern and Southwestern population centers are growing.

Where market decline is gradual and unnoticed, the newspaper serving the area may slip, too, despite all efforts. It may appear that the newspaper's sag in circulation and ad volume is attributable to some shortcoming on the part of management and other employes, while the real cause is a change in market size and composition.

Conversely, if the market is in a period of runaway growth—as in many suburbs during the post-World War II population explosion—a newspaper may seem to be turning in a virtuoso performance. In reality, the paper may be showing less improvement than is warranted by the influx of additional people and economic activity.

Thus the operation of a newspaper, and the evaluation of its performance, should not be conducted in a vacuum. Both must be considered against the background of the ever-changing local market.

Although newspapers are dependent upon the economic health of their markets, few participate vigorously in efforts to maintain them. Some editors believe strongly that a newspaper's role is to observe and report to its market, not to be an active participant in it.

This attitude is changing in some cases. One prominent newspaper publisher, chairman of the board of his company and a past chairman of the American Newspaper Publishers Association, summed up the view: "If we are responsible newspapers, we should not merely be IN the community, we should be PART of the community."[9]

Another publisher, a former editor, elaborated: "Our newspapers live in the cities that sustain us, and we have an obligation to see that these communities become better places to live, helping our readers achieve those basic human rights and aspirations that we all share. That means we offer the encouragement along with the criticism, we provide the ideas, the motivation, the information and the editorial leadership for improvement."[10]

Because of their ability to gather, interpret, store and retrieve news, newspapers are in an unsurpassed position to sense incipient trends in the communities they serve—trends in changing population components, housing concentration and dispersal, retail sales and other elements important to the economic health of the community.

Without compromising independence to cover the news as reporters and editors see it, both small and large newspapers increasingly are alerting their communities to economic opportunities and dangers; helping attract additional businesses to their towns to provide employment and missing services and to make their communities' economics less dependent upon the fortunes of a few enterprises. That way, newspapers perform a useful community service in ways that benefit the newspaper as well.

In summary, the trend is away from the unyielding perception of the newspaper as an isolated, self-sufficient entity as depicted in Figure 1. Increasingly the newspaper is recognized as a reciprocating part of its market as in Figure 2.

The outer rings represent the market served by the newspaper. Every individual in the market, regardless of age, sex, education or other characteristics, is categorized as a reader or nonreader. Similarly, every business either is or is not an advertiser.

The size of each ring segment is proportionate to the number of cases represented. The newspaper shown here has few competing media and, as indicated by arrows, is in continuing contact with its readers and advertisers. It also reaches nonreaders and nonadvertisers through advertising and circulation solicitations, editorial contacts and promotional messages.

How the Newspaper Functions

Generations of journalism students have been told that newspapers serve by enlightening, informing, entertaining and protecting the community, by exposing malefactors and by serving as the medium of record.

Students of an earlier generation also were told that newspapers "mold public opinion." This is not precisely true, as almost any editorial

Figure 2
The Market

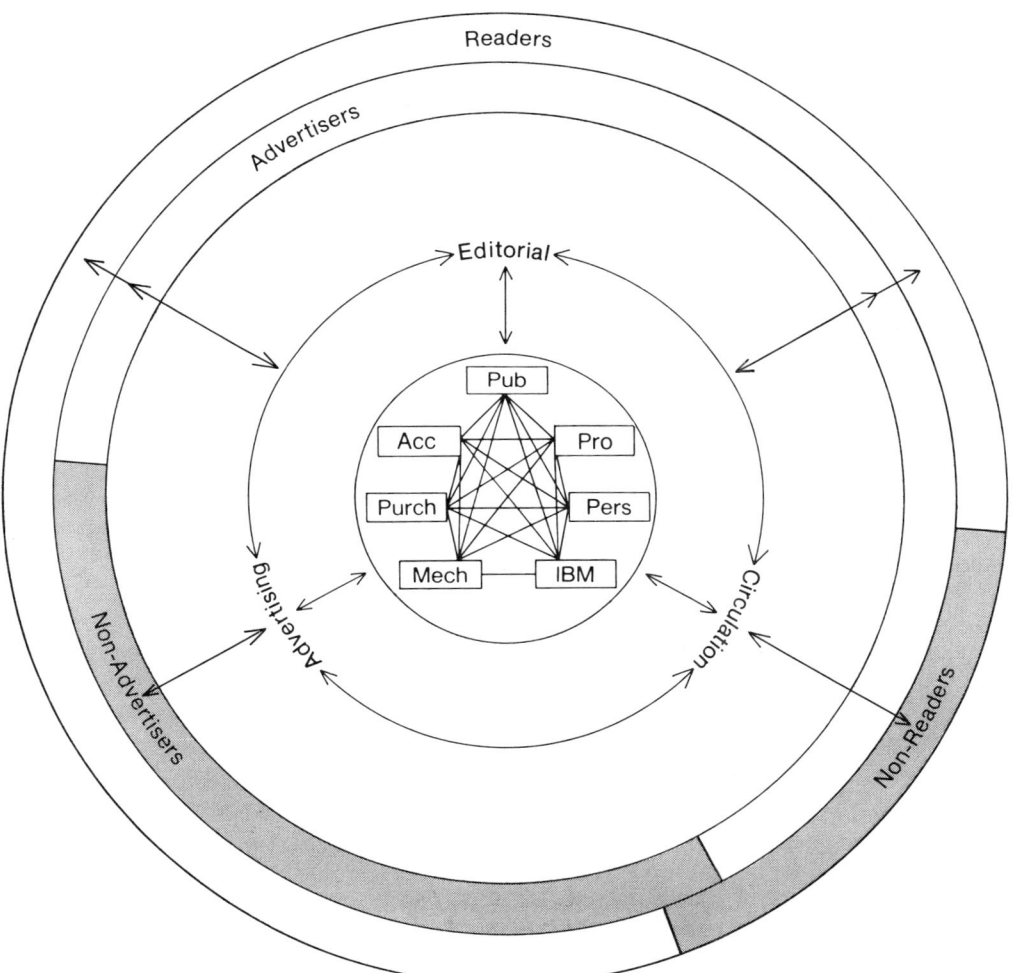

writer will tell you as he surveys his list of losers the morning after almost any election. And in this day of disenchantment with anything resembling manipulation, the notion that newspapers "mold" public opinion is calculated to make people resent them. In reality, newspapers are a means toward achieving social consensus. Two factors are involved: The newspaper's presentation of a broad spectrum of relevant facts on specific issues, and its ability to reach significant numbers of people in all segments of society.

The mechanics of the second factor are not well understood, even by some newspaper people. Yet the consensus-generating function is a critically important activity deserving of its First Amendment protections. Also, an understanding of consensus building helps a newspaper better structure itself to reach its marketplace and to broaden its utility to the reader.

The Case for Consensus

Through objective presentation of fact and opinion, newspapers serve as a lubricant in the gearbox of society, helping it to shift gears in adjusting to changing conditions. In recent years these have often been sudden, jolting shifts of great magnitude, such as that produced by the Arab oil embargo of late 1973.

By alerting people to new issues and by providing a forum for all points of view, a newspaper prepares its readers for incipient change and fosters consensus on the amount and kind of change a community will tolerate.

The great value of this social service became apparent with the swift and dramatic changes in recent years from traditional attitudes about youth, women, blacks, sex, abortion, ecology, church authority, government accountability and corporations' social responsibility.

In countries without a free press, demand for change is often marked by repression followed by revolt. A free society with good newspapers has other, better options.

Yet, editors do not regard consensus building as their prime mission, nor should they. This social contribution is a happy byproduct of covering news properly and of reaching the maximum audience.

As a past-president of the Associated Press Managing Editors Association recently stated, "We need newspapers not just to report our communities, but to provide a means for our communities to report themselves. We need to be more of a soapbox, more of a bulletin board. We need to give readers information while it is still in the making, to be informed participants in government. People need to be alerted so that they can react and even more, contribute, to the discussions of public matters before they are all decided."[11]

This is a subtle shift in emphasis from thinking of "communication" as a flow of information only *from* newspaper *to* reader.

It is not clear whether newspapers will meet the challenge of helping build a consensus on the energy crisis; inflation; the dwindling supplies of some raw materials; municipal fiscal crises, and faltering institutions such as Penn Central and the Social Security System.

Columnist Joseph Kraft has noted how decisively Congress acts when the national mind is made up, but how it ducks problems when no consensus for action has crystallized. He calls the latter "a coalition of paralysis."[12]

Only the free newspaper offers society an opportunity to develop issues in breadth and depth on a continuing basis, reflecting local sentiments, all packaged in a form available at the reader's convenience on a regular basis.

Readers are looking for ways to have their views represented in the reshaping of their society. Thus, the press has an opportunity to enlarge its role to what the general manager of the American Newspaper Publishers Association has described as "a nation-building, *consensusforming* institution that rallies the people behind shared national goals."[13]

To do this, newspapers must maintain truthfulness, courage, impartiality and equal zeal in presenting all points of view, pro and con, across the social spectrum of rich and poor, young and old, white and black, blue collar, white collar and no collar. And, newspapers must "reach" all those segments of their market.

Many assume that because newspapers are a "mass medium," they automatically have all the reach needed to cover everyone. This is far from the case. For example, the top line of Figure 3 shows the distribution of adults by education in one U.S. market. The dotted line shows the relative coverage of each group in the market by one local newspaper. Note the lack of total market penetration and the relatively heavy concentration of readership in the best educated group.

Figure 4 presents a picture of the same market and the coverage pattern of a competing newspaper. Note the differences in reader profile resulting from differences in editorial content, emphasis and presentation.

Contrast the two previous examples with the newspaper illustrated in Figure 5 serving a *different* market:

Note the generally higher levels of coverage across the market of the latter newspaper, and its deeper penetration into each group. This newspaper, because of its more universal reach, has the ability to function more effectively than either of the other two both as a mechanism for consensus and as an advertising vehicle. It has "depth" of readership that will make the newspaper productive for every category of advertiser and useful as a forum for exchange of community news and views.

No newspaper is "all things to all people," and it never can be. But

Figure 3
MARKET PENETRATION BY EDUCATION, NEWSPAPER A

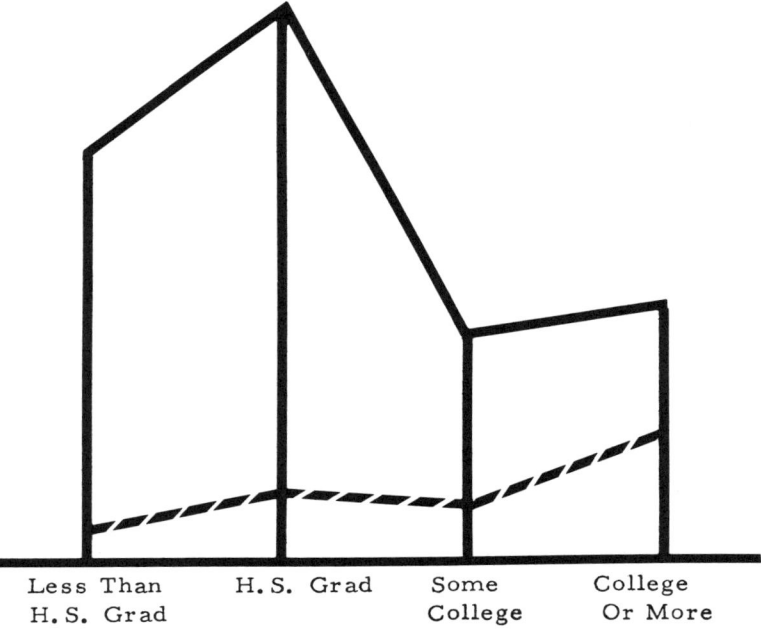

Figure 4
MARKET PENETRATION BY EDUCATION, NEWSPAPER B

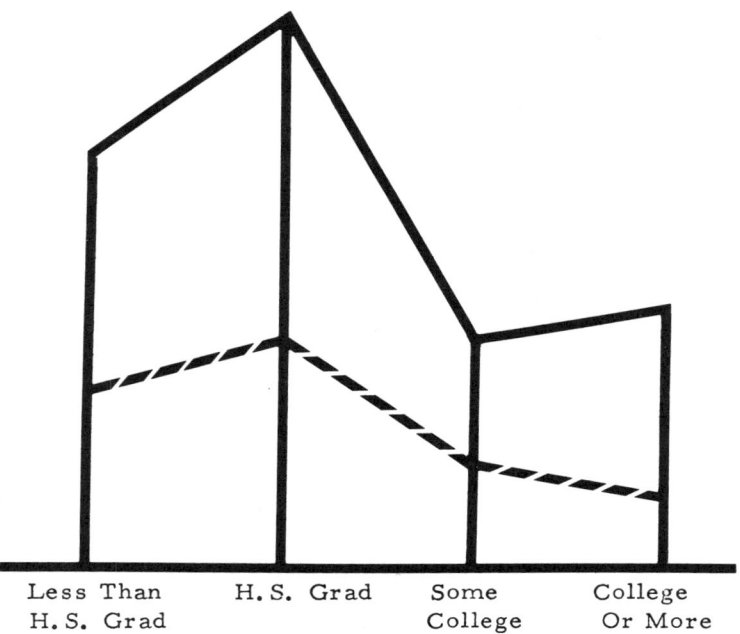

Figure 5
MARKET PENETRATION BY EDUCATION, NEWSPAPER C

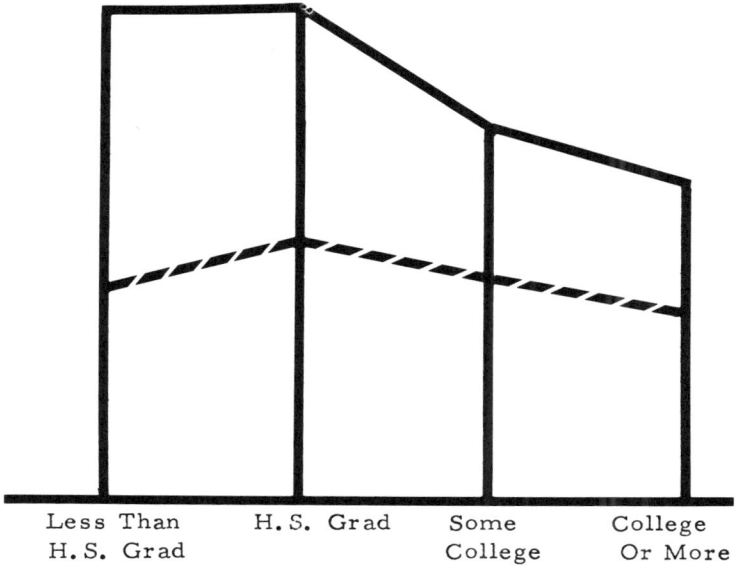

each newspaper offers something of compelling interest to substantial numbers in every demographic group. Most newspapers feel their goal should be to build on that base and to expand readership in categories that are underrepresented.

The goal can be attained through purposeful editing, special features appealing to a wide variety of interest groups and an emphasis on circulation development in underrepresented segments of the primary market area. One big-city newspaper was able to increase its coverage of young adult readers by 50 percent in three years. That kind of "audience tuning" can make newspapers more profitable, as well as more effective instruments of social dialogue.

In short, a newspaper's editorial content effects not only the kind and amount of readership it attracts, but also the kind and amount of advertising it will carry. Thus editorial and advertising departments share a common need far removed from the age-old editorial fear of puffery or favored news treatment for big advertisers. Both departments need audience breadth and depth—the editorial department to reflect the opinions and interests of the whole community; the ad department to carry the messages of advertisers to the whole community. This shared need is represented by a two-headed arrow in organizational diagrams. (See Figure 2.)

The Importance of the Editorial Function

The importance of news reporting and other editorial activities is obvious in the title "newspaper." Journalism "is a profession which depends on and exists for the fulfillment of a particular desire that is as old as man—the desire to have the news."[14] Without the editorial function, a printed document is not a newspaper.

Unless the editorial product is of high quality, the newspaper is not fulfilling its obligations to its community or the First Amendment and is not achieving its full potential as a business enterprise.

Advertising is Also a Reader Service

In spite of occasional grumbling about "too much advertising," readers do want it in their newspapers. The reason is simple.

Newspaper advertising is a current, daily directory of goods and services. It lets the community know what's in style, in season and in stock and who offers it at what price. It enables the reader to shop and compare without leaving the home, and to get good value for the dollars he or she has worked hard to earn.

Many readers will not buy a newspaper with little advertising content or advertising not meeting their needs. But, wise newspapers do not simply turn ad salesmen loose to sell all the ads they can to whatever merchants will buy them. It is usually more productive to develop additional advertising in key geographic, merchandise type and price areas where the newspaper is underrepresented for important concentrations of potential readers.

What the Advertising Department Sells

Ask any newsman what the ad department sells. He probably will tell you, "Space."

In reality what is sold is *not* space, but response. The advertiser is interested only in the number of sales that space will produce for him, and what it costs. If an editorial product has distribution and representative appeal to the whole market, advertising response is likely to be satisfactory for all types of consumer goods and services.

"Deep and broad" circulation are important to the advertiser because the market for any particular item of merchandise is quite thin on a given day. A specific example is women's hosiery, one of the items most frequently purchased by women. Yet less than two percent buy hosiery on an average shopping day.[15] If the same item is offered by several advertisers on the same day, a newspaper must reach a broad audience or it cannot produce enough response to justify the ads.

Advertising's Contribution to the Editorial Department

Advertising typically generates the bulk of revenue required to support a paper.[16] It also contributes substantially to reader interest and circulation. Over the years, reader studies have shown that some advertising content is as well read as some editorial content.[17] A newspaper often is as eagerly awaited for its advertising as for its news.

People work hard to earn money for the things they want. So it makes sense for a newspaper to offer features as well as ads discussing the things readers' want—*when they want them most.*

Department stores list approximately 90 different standard product categories. Seasonal changes in public interest in each of them are reflected in various sales and advertising volume reports. Each product class has its own sales and advertising pattern reflecting customer demand.

As Figure 6 demonstrates, consumers are interested in different products at different times of the year. It is during periods of peak interest that readers particularly welcome and value editorial guidance and shopping information.

Some ad departments make available to feature editors information on the ebb and flow of advertising of fashions, furniture, home furnishings and other products. When *editors* use such information as a guide to timing and nature of features, they also produce a newspaper of recognizably greater interest and use to readers.

Circulation's Contribution to the Newspaper

If advertising and editorial departments are coordinated in their effort to serve the reader, they can be of immense help in providing the circulation department with a saleable product—a newspaper containing the proper amounts, kinds and balance of news and advertising that appeal to existing and potential subscribers. (This interrelationship is recognized in Figure 2.)

The circulation department reciprocates by maintaining its current distribution and by focusing promotional activities in areas where the editorial and advertising departments are concentrating their mutual efforts toward growth and utility.

Little purpose is served by the editorial and ad departments working cooperatively toward building reader interest in Area A if the circula-

Figure 6
DISTRIBUTION OF ADVERTISING FOR TWO COMMODITIES IN THE PHOENIX, ARIZONA MARKET

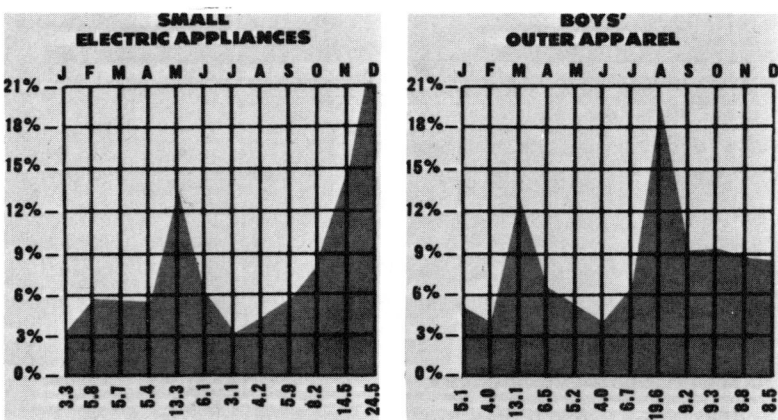

Source: "Inside Phoenix," 1971, Arizona Gazette

tion department is busy getting subscriptions in Area Z because "Area Z is easier to work." This sort of situation is not uncommon under the standard pyramidal organization pattern.

Circulation goals consistent with the marketing concept include:

Procurement: Emphasize achieving optimum depth and breadth of reader mix to sustain advertising response and editorial content.
Retention: Try to retain subscribers moving to new locations in the same town, and improve service and collection techniques to avoid cancellations.
Replacement: Discontinue unprofitable service to remote areas and step up efforts to offset those circulation losses by obtaining new readers in more central locations.

To summarize, circulation departments increasingly are concerning themselves not only with circulation numbers, but with the kinds and locations of readers they must serve to help newspapers fulfill their editorial and advertising missions.

Completing the Structure

One alternative to the historic, hierarchal newspaper structure positions the editorial, advertising and circulation departments as *customer-responsive* and interdependent entities. Other newspaper departments serve whichever of the major three needs help. The two inner circles of Figure 2 present a picture of the teamwork and communication flow among the various operating departments of a newspaper and its market.

Each department consists of specialists. And each retains autonomy in its area of expertise but operating decisions are made with full knowledge of the newspaper's overall goals and objectives *and* the activities of other departments. With proper orientation and coordination, a newspaper is better organized to meet readers' and advertisers' needs and to earn a profit.

Alternative Views

In the newspaper business, with all its divergent points of view, it is not surprising that an evolving philosophy is not universally shared.

Some editors already are enthusiastic proponents of the marketing concept. "What newspapers need to discover," said one, "is who their readers are, what they want, and make the obvious changes."[18]

Other editors see the marketing concept as an encroachment upon their independence. They are adamant in their refusal to "abrogate their coverage of the news" to make their columns "responsive" to reader wishes. They suspect readers might demand slant in news presentation, bringing the marketing concept and objective journalism into direct conflict. Some editors believe, as one said: "The newspaper is an institution that sets out to do more than just maximize its market. The newspaper is a quasi-public institution with a constitutional purpose . . . The press has never been and never should be in business to give people just what they want. An editor who does his editing *predominantly* from market research returns isn't worth a damn."[19]

The key word is "predominantly." Most editors already routinely implement the marketing concept—without calling it that—to the degree that they keep abreast of developing reader interest in such feature areas as sports, leisure activities, the arts and so on. They try to balance the amount and variety of such coverage in each issue to appeal to a majority of readers.

Webster defined news in part as "matter which is newsworthy." Newsworthy is defined as "sufficiently interesting to the general public to warrant reporting (as in a newspaper)."[20] According to that definition, it is the public that ultimately determines what is newsworthy.

On the other hand, nothing in the marketing concept suggests that a newspaper avoid coverage of an event or issue which *should be* of interest to its readers. Providing information and creating concern over a significant issue about which the public is unaware or apathetic is an important function of the newspaper. The marketing concept recognizes that market research to determine reader interests is not the sole determinant of the content of the newspaper. The concept is a philosophy of business that emphasizes customer *needs and desires* in the creation and delivery of a product or service. The public needs to know the news and desires information appealing to its interests.

There are those who object to the idea that a newspaper should seek more representative distribution in its market. Some general newspapers historically have readership concentrated in one part of the spectrum, which they have come to regard as "their niche." Other newspapers such as the *Wall Street Journal* are, by design, specialized publications serving a specific segment of the market. This is in no way contrary to the marketing concept because the concept does not suggest that every business must seek to serve *all* consumers. However, the objection to representative distribution does run counter to the appeal for consensus. Some observers believe that concentrating on consensus may lead a newspaper to take too strong a position on a critical issue, rather than serving as a medium for information and dialogue. Ironically many suspect that the opposite is true; that in fostering consensus a newspaper might avoid a specific stand on an issue.

Conclusion

Whether or not every detail of a newspaper's role in fostering consensus is accepted, the marketing concept and plain common sense require a newspaper to define its intended market and then attempt to serve that market effectively. To achieve that purpose, coordination among the various departments and functions of a newspaper is essential.

The "total newspaper" is not editorial brilliance alone, not just advertising excellence, not circulation expertise by itself. It is an interacting, editorial-advertising-production circulation operation applied to a specific geographic, demographic and economic base—the market the newspaper serves.[21]

As one commentator states, "It is old-fashioned to believe that a newspaper is put together by a series of independent and isolated entrepreneurs in the editorial, advertising and circulation departments who meet only at the front and back ends of the printing press. . . . Understanding, cooperation and coordination of these departments is the name of the game today."[22]

With an understanding of ever-changing markets and with departmental teamwork, newspapers can flourish in an age of rapidly changing technology and life styles.

NOTES
Chapter 3

[1] Jon G. Udell and Gene R. Laczniak, *Marketing in a Dynamic Society* (New York, N.Y.: Harcourt Brace Jovanovich, Inc., forthcoming 1979).

[2] See Thomas L. Berg, *Mismarketing: Case Histories of Marketing Misfires* (New York, N.Y.: Doubleday and Company, 1970).

[3] Mobility of U.S. Population, 1970–74. Report P20-273, U.S. Dept. of Commerce, Bureau of Census.

[4] Charles Bennett, *Facts Without Opinion*, Chicago, Ill.: Audit Bureau of Circulation, 1905.

[5] Theodore Levitt, "Marketing Myopia," *Harvard Business Review* (September–October 1975).

[6] January 31, 1973, Enclosure to ANPA Newsletter.

[7] Martin Northway, December 1974, Hyde Parker Magazine, *The Tribune Story*.

[8] Classified-Retail Ad Sales: Cooperation or Competition, September 27, 1975, *Editor & Publisher*.

[9] Davis Taylor, May 1975, Speech to the International Newspaper Promotion Association Conference, Mexico City.

[10] Don Carter, The Press—*Its Changing Mission*, Sigma Delta Chi Foundation Lecture, University of Colorado, Nov. 19, 1974.

[11] Richard D. Smyser, Speech to the 16th Annual Public Relations Society of America Institute, July 11, 1974.

[12] Joseph Kraft, "Coalition of Paralysis Poorly Governs America," June 25, 1975, Chicago *Daily News* (syndicated column).

[13] I. William Hill, September 13, 1975, *Editor & Publisher*, "Jerry W. Friedheim sets ANPA Priorities."

[14] William H. Hornby, "Beware the 'Market' Thinkers . . . Are Newspapers Forgetting They're in the *NEWS* Business?", *The Quill*, January 1976, p. 16.

[15] Newspaper Advertising Bureau study for Newsprint Information Committee, 633 Third Avenue, New York, N.Y. 10017, 1975, *Shoppers on the Move*.

[16] For a more complete discussion of advertising revenue see Chapter 7.

[17] Carl J. Nelson Research, Inc., Chicago, Illinois.

[18] Mike Davies, managing editor of the Louisville (Ky.) *Times*, quoted in Content, Presentation Changes Urged, *Editor & Publisher*, January 31, 1976.

[19] William H. Hornby, *op. cit.*

[20] *Webster's New Collegiate Dictionary*, G. & C. Merriam Company, Springfield, Massachusetts, 1974.

[21] Foreword, *Promoting the Total Newspaper*, 1974. International Newspaper Promotion Association, Dulles International Airport, P. O. Box 17422, Washington, D.C. 20041.

[22] Editorial, May 18, 1974, *Editor & Publisher*.

4

Understanding Profit in the Newspaper Business

AMERICAN NEWSPAPERS are consumer and industrial producers[1] subject to the same economic laws influencing any other business in a free society. Newspapers must satisfy their customers and, in the process, generate sufficient revenues to remain in business. As Robert G. Marbut, president and chief executive officer of Harte-Hanks Communications, Inc. has said, "These two things—a product that satisfies customers and a profit that provides a return—are fundamental to any business, and newspapers are no exception."[2]

The Profit Controversy

Profits are basic to success of a business enterprise. But of all the dimensions of American Industry, profit is perhaps the most misunderstood and debated.

The profitability of newspapers sometimes receives special attention because newspapers enjoy the privileges and responsibilities of the First Amendment. In fact, some view newspapers as quasi-public institutions. Indeed, most newspaper organizations, and particularly editorial employes, insist that their line of work represents a high form of public service. Warren H. Phillips, former reporter and now president of Dow Jones & Co., Inc. (publisher of *The Wall Street Journal* and other newspapers) pointed out, "Dow Jones' reason for existing, and the motivation behind everything we do, is to strengthen the service our publications and newswires perform for our society. It's almost impossible to exaggerate the contribution that our joint efforts make each day to a better informed business community and public at large. This in turn hopefully enables wiser decisions to be made to advance the country's economic, political and social welfare."[3]

While U.S. newspapers function as public servants, they do so as private enterprises and this casts them in a dual role. Media critic Ben Bagdikian put it this way: "On the one hand, the daily paper in the United States is a product of professionals whose reporting is supposed to be the result of disciplined intelligence gathering and analysis in order to present an honest and understandable picture of the social and political world. If this reportage is in any way influenced by concern for money-making it is regarded as corrupt journalism. On the other hand, the American daily newspaper . . . has to remain solvent and has to make a profit or else it will not survive. If it doesn't make money there will be no reporting of any kind, ethical or unethical. If the corporate end of the enterprise does not have an effective concern for making money it will be regarded by everyone, including journalists, as incompetent, negligent and a disservice to its community."[4]

This "split personality" of the business often creates tension between editorial and business offices. News executives and reporters are primarily concerned with producing a quality editorial product. For this reason they tend to hold the business side of the paper at arm's length for fear of possible interference. For example, a study of a leading U.S. newspaper shows that some news executives are naturally suspicious of their business colleagues and the money-making function of the paper.[5]

This attitude stems in large part from a journalist's training which stresses skepticism as an attribute. Revelations of questionable and illegal business practices sharpen such an attitude. Arthur R. Taylor, former president of CBS, Inc., points out that business executives often complain that reporters are biased against private enterprise and the profit-reward system. He adds, however, "I think that reporters simply mirror the general public's fundamental lack of understanding and its consequent mistrust of the free enterprise system."[6] Although the editorial-business office relationship may not be close, most editors realize that their desire for a quality product eventually translates into calls for a bigger news department budget. For this and other reasons, editors cannot be completely independent of business considerations. However, this does not mean that their coverage of the news must be influenced by business considerations.

Most publishers are no less concerned with quality than their editorial employes. But they and their business managers must also meet payrolls, pay bills, finance new equipment and budget for the advertising, production and circulation departments whose officials also frequently clamor for more funds to meet rising costs and improve services.

Proving that newspaper quality and earnings are highly interrelated is difficult because earnings are the product of many factors, not just editorial excellence. Organizational efficiency and the nature of the market served are major determinants of profitability (see Chapter 3) to say nothing of competition within the market.

However, the role of product quality in business success or failure has been demonstrated in many industries. Most newspaper executives agree with *Washington Post*'s executive editor Benjamin C. Bradlee that "excellence is profitability." A more detailed examination of product quality and profitability is presented in Chapter 5.

The Role of Profit

The gap between editorial and business views of profit is narrowed by a general recognition that a newspaper must be independent editorially and economically. John Colburn, publisher of *The Californian* in El Cajon, Calif., has stated: "Editorial independence, protected by the First Amendment against government control, gives newspapers in the United States strength and influence unmatched in the world. It is economic independence, though, that provides newspapers with a strong bulwark to resist pressures from politicians, government bureaucrats, advertisers and special interest groups."[7] A similar view was expressed by Otis Chandler, vice chairman of the Times Mirror Company and publisher of *The Los Angeles Times*, "You cannot have a good editorial product or provide community service unless you have good profits."[8]

The view that profits are essential to business success is fundamental in a free enterprise economy. In a free economic system, the forces of supply and demand determine prices and allocate resources. Profits are viewed as an incentive for investment and participation in the system. This incentive is highly important because a free market economy relies primarily on the initiative of individuals and groups of individuals, rather than on government. Profits are seen as the reward or "carrot," while losses are the penalty or "stick" for failing to serve society.

Blessings and Evils of Profit

Profits and the profit motive stir emotions. They conjure up moral as well as economic issues and generally are viewed as a great blessing by some and a great evil by others.

Most businessmen, including publishers, will tell you that profits are necessary to attract and reward capital, motivate entrepreneurs, improve the product, provide jobs and retire debt. They may also explain that profits are in fact a "cost"—a price that must be paid to attract the capital necessary to produce a newspaper. On the other hand, some workers and certain political activists will tell you that profits are exploitative and that profit makers tend to be greedy and insensitive to the others' needs. Opponents of profit usually argue that it results from underpayment of labor or overcharging of consumers.

The proponents of free enterprise point out that profit incentives and retained earnings have enabled the United States, in its short history, to achieve a phenomenal standard of living. They believe profits are fully compatible with social well being. Certainly the profit motive has led to the establishment of small and large business enterprises—including newspapers—that provide employment, technological advances which increase productivity, and many valuable products and services. In his book *Understanding Profits,* Claude Robinson points out that profits: "(1) motivate men to undetake economic activity that is useful to the community; (2) reward the risktakers for saving capital and putting it to work in productive jobs; (3) provide a mechanism for social control, both for management and the consuming public, in allocating labor and resources to the jobs society wants done."[9]

On the other hand, profits often are vilified as the height of selfishness and as a brutalizing force placing wealth above humanity and efficiency over social justice. For example, in criticizing landlords' profits, some tenants claim "housing is for living, not for profit."

Some antagonism toward profit arises from misconceptions about the actual profitability of American industry. A recent poll by Opinion Research Corporation reveals that the general public estimates that industry makes over 30 percent profit after taxes on each dollar of sales. The actual average for many years has been around 5 percent.

Explanations of Profit

Most contrasting views concerning profits and their role in society spring from the diverse nature of four major profit theories: the "compensatory," "friction and monopoly," "exploitation of labor" and "innovation" theories.

According to the compensatory theory, profits either are payments to entrepreneurs for successful management or a reward for taking financial risks. In the friction and monopoloy theory, profit is the economic result of collusion among a number of firms or the control of production by one firm that uses its monopoloy position to exploit consumers. Under the exploitation of labor theory (that of Karl Marx) profits are said to result from underpaying workers whose labor alone determines the value of the commodity produced. The innovation theory broadly visualizes profit as the reward, and the incentive, for successfully introducing a new product or method of production.[10]

All four have some merit; and, with the exception of the exploitation of labor theory, they are similar in some respects. For instance, the conceptions of profits as a compensation for management and risk taking and as a reward for successful innovation are closely allied. The U.S. government has recognized the merit of each theory by enacting patent and copyright laws to spur innovation; anti-trust laws to curb monopoly and foster competition, unfair labor standards and minimum wage laws to prevent the exploitation of labor, and investment credits to stimulate risk taking and investment.

Whether a profit is a blessing or an evil depends upon how it is earned. If a business profits by efficiently and honestly serving customers in a competitive marketplace, its profit cannot be viewed as evil. If a significant share of profits are devoted to providing new or improved products and additional employment, the social benefits of profit are enhanced. It is of interest that at one time the profits of newspapers were the primary economic base for the development of a new and major medium of communication and entertainment—television. For the most part, other potential investors were unwilling to risk their capital in the then infant and uncertain television industry.

Profit: A Cost

Unfortunately, none of the more prominantly recognized profit theories adequately recognizes that, up to a point, profits are a cost.

There are three major factors in production—land (including other natural resources), labor and capital. Except where a factor is so abundant that it has no "scarcity" value, it must be compensated. For example, a new newspaper plant requires a multi-million dollar investment. That portion of the capital which is borrowed has a clear cost—the interest on the indebtedness. The equity capital invested in the facility must at least have a promise of reward—potential profit. Profit is the compensation for capital. Investors in a newspaper expect a return on their investment, just as Mary Jones expects interest on her federally insured savings deposit.

In his book, *The Age of Discontinuity,* Peter Drucker viewed profit as a future cost. He said the main question concerning profits "is whether they are high enough to allow the economy to take the risks it needs to take in order to grow." These costs, said Drucker, "cannot yet be measured, but they are as real, as tangible and as certain as the costs of the past that our accounts record. Just as we ask with respect to the costs of the past whether there is enough revenue to cover them, we must ask with respect to the costs of the future whether there is enough revenue to cover them."[11]

The New York Stock Exhange has projected that there may not be enough capital around to cover future costs. In 1974 it pointed out that domestic capital needs through 1985—including those of governments at all levels—could exceed the available supply of savings by $650 billion. James Needham, former Exchange chairman, stated that any shortage "would be evident in rising interest rates—prompted by intensifying competition for an inadequate supply of savings—and by reduced credit availability to all but the strongest borrowers."[12] Therefore, the level of profits among private business enterprises—perhaps as never before—will determine future borrowing strength in capital markets. And, of course, industry will be competing with the strongest U.S. borrower, the federal government.

Another exchange study of capital needs, conducted in 1975, pointed to a "serious deterioration in corporate balance sheet positions."[13] It projected that over the next decade U.S. corporations—including newspapers—will need to raise $250 billion through new equity funding. The exchange suggested programs "focused on tax incentives to stimulate the resurgence of individual investment by Americans" to head off a capital crunch.[14]

The outlook for most newspapers in a capital-short market, however, appears fairly good. Evidence indicates that the daily newspaper business is fairly profitable. While financial analysts have varying views of the future, most are optimistic that newspaper profits will increase as the result of technological advances in the communications industry (a subject of Chapter 10).

The Profitability of Newspapers

Most of the 1,762 U.S. daily newspapers—about 1,500—are privately owned and under no obligation to reveal their earnings. However, approximately 250 daily newspapers are owned by companies that sell their stock to the public and issue public financial statements. Analysts believe that profits of well-managed privately owned dailies and of publicly owned newspapers differ little.[15]

John Morton, a newspaper financial analyst for Colin, Hochstin Company, closely follows the records of 13 of the 22 publicly owned newspaper companies. These companies publish about 200 daily newspapers that account for 21 percent of U.S. daily circulation.[16] Most of those public companies also own television and radio stations and some publish weekly newspapers and magazines and have subsidaries engaged in diverse media-related activities such as book publishing and newsprint production. Therefore, the profitability of their newspapers cannot always be exactly determined.

Morton calculated that in 1976 the after-tax profit margins of the 13 newspaper companies he studies averaged 10 percent of sales.[17] This was substantially more than the 5.5 percent after-tax return on sales of all manufacturers of durable and nondurable goods for the same period[18]—a difference indicating relatively good financial and management health, at least among publicly held newspapers. After-tax margins on the income of individual newspaper companies in 1976 ranged from a low of 4.4 percent to a high of 17 percent. For the past five years, after-tax margins of the 13 companies averaged 9.3 percent of sales income. Morton estimated that the pre-tax margins of 12 of the 13 (one could not be computed) averaged 18.4 percent over the five-year period. Apparently, almost one-half of newspapers' before-tax income is absorbed by federal and state income taxes.

Estimates of Edward Dunleavy, an analyst covering the newspaper business for Merrill Lynch Pierce Fenner & Smith, Inc. also indicate financial health among newspapers. Prior to 1969, revenue and pre-tax profits for the printing and publishing industry reported to the Federal Trade Commission and the Securities and Exchange Commission excluded newspapers. With newspaper profits included in printing and publishing industry reports in 1969, the pre-tax profit margin of printing and publishing companies rose from 7.8 percent in 1968 to 9 percent. Dunleavy said, ". . . distinct improvement in pre-tax profit margins . . . in 1969 supports our estimate that the newspaper industry has higher profit margins than does the entire printing and publishing industry."[19]

The newspaper business requires an unusually large investment (relative to sales) in plant and equipment. Therefore, to remain financially sound, newspapers must earn a fairly high return on sales. Profits *cannot* be properly evaluated only as a percent of sales—*it is return on equity* (the investment of owners) that really counts.

Return on Equity

Unfortunately, little information on newspapers' return on equity is available, except for the publicly owned companies. In 1976, the return on stockholders' equity of 13 publically held companies averaged 16.0 percent; the range of individual companies was from a low of 11.9 percent to a high of 24.0 percent.

From this and other data several conclusions are evident:

- Many newspapers earn a return on equity that is comparable to or higher than the average of all manufacturing industry. As a result several new newspapers are founded each year and there are now as many U.S. dailies as there were in 1946. Profitability enables newspapers to make substantial capital investments, over $250 million annually.
- Not all newspapers earn an adequate return on equity. As a result, several dailies perish each year, while others continue to struggle for survival. In addition, several newspapers remain in business only because of the financial support of other commonly owned enterprises, such as television stations, or because previously accumulated earnings provide a financial cushion during periods of economic losses.
- Profit potential is reduced when there is more than one daily newspaper in a community. Consequently, most U.S. communities have only one locally published daily newspaper. However, in one-newspaper towns there usually are at least several other news outlets available to the public, such as radio or television stations, specialized publications, weeklies and the newspapers of other nearby communities. Some communities have more than one daily—they may be morning and afternoon papers owned by the same company or independently owned dailies—because of their large populations. In 22 cities there are joint operating agreements between two local newspapers that are separately owned, one of which was considered to be failing at the time of the arrangement. These agreements, sanctioned by Congress in the Newspaper Preservation Act of 1970, authorize newspapers to combine their business and production operations while maintaining separate news organizations. Opponents say such arrangements curtail competition and make it impossible for an alternate daily to survive or enter the market. Proponents say the agreements preserve two competing newspaper editorial voices in the community.
- The average return on invested capital of all U.S. corporations, especially manufacturers, has been relatively low in recent years. As shown in Figure 1, return on capital invested, including borrowed capital, fell below 5 percent in 1974. Yet, some of the borrowed capital involved cost industry well over 10 percent. Five percent is hardly an ade-

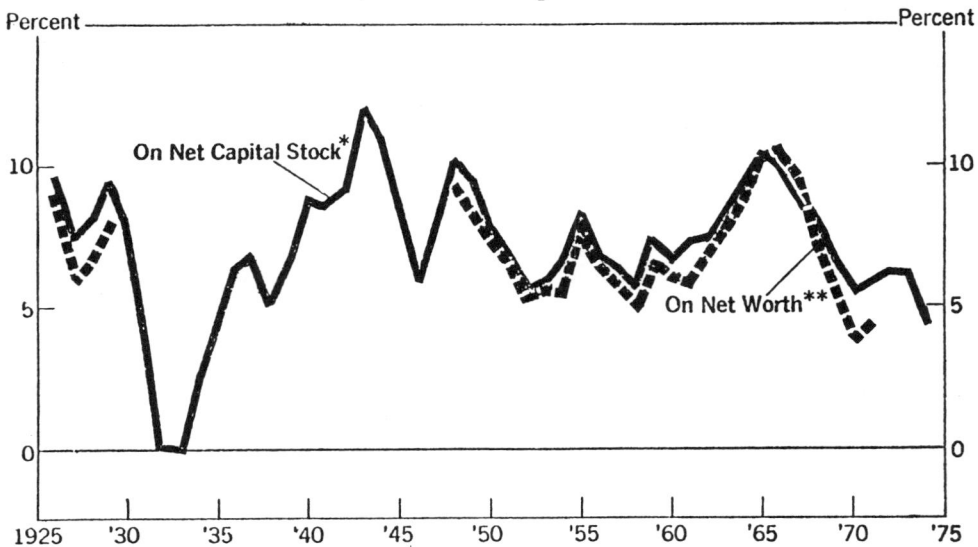

**Figure 1
RETURN ON CAPITAL
Nonfinancial Corporations**

* Profits after tax plus interest as a percent of depreciated capital stock including inventories.
** Profits after tax as percent of Net Profits, Net Capital Stock and Net Worth have been adjusted to current price valuation of assets and constant depreciation (straight line) based on 85 percent of Bulletin F. Lines.
Source: U.S. Department of the Treasury.

quate reward for assuming the risks of business ownership in inflationary times when far more secure and attractive returns, such as interest on government bonds, are available elsewhere. The 13 publicly owned newspaper companies, however, averaged a 12.5 percent return on invested capital in 1974.

Are Newspaper Profits "Reasonable"?

Ascertaining whether newspaper or other business profits are reasonable, too high or too low is difficult and highly subjective. The rate of return on equity investment should be sufficient to reward investors fairly, insure the future quality of the newspaper and attract further investments when they are needed. That return should exceed the rate of inflation so that investors do not suffer a "real" loss in the value of their investment over time. To be attractive, the rate of return on equity, with its many risks, certainly should exceed interest from a relatively unrisky investment in a federally insured bank or from a savings and loan deposit. Currently, six-year certificates of deposit earn an annual rate of around 8 percent.

Business management often views profit rates in terms of what a company should earn, given its market potential, its stage of development and resources available, and the intensity of competition. As the publisher of a thriving Georgia daily asked, "Is the newspaper in the developmental stages of reaching the market? Or has the paper matured to the point that it has taught all the folks to read it might hope to and has done a competent job of selling its advertising and meeting competition?"[20] Otis Chandler of the Times Mirror Co. has pointed out, "Generally. . . . for most small and medium-size newspapers, a 15 percent after-tax profit (on sales) would be a reasonable goal. For a metropolitan newspaper an 8 percent . . . goal would be reasonable."[21]

From a social point of view, a reasonable profit is that which will protect the economic and editorial viability of the newspaper. A lesser amount would endanger both employes and the paper's service to the public. A greater amount over a sustained period of time would be exploitative. At one time, when there was little inflation, a 5 percent return on equity might have been viewed as socially reasonable. Today, because of inflation, owners would have less value (including profits) at the end of the year than at the beginning with only 5 percent return of equity. Public service commissions frequently adopt a 12 percent target rate of return for the utilities they regulate. Given the social importance of the free press' economic health and the risks of failure, most newspapers should earn at least that amount and perhaps more. The question of reasonable profit for newspapers will be explored further in the next chapter.

Profit Problems of the Press

As suggested by the demise of many newspapers over the years, some dailies have had insurmountable profit problems. A major source of current problems is high inflation which has hit newspapers unusually hard. While newspapers have lower material cost, as a percentage of all costs, than most manufacturing industries, newsprint runs as high as 30 percent of a large newspaper's total costs. The price of newsprint per ton soared almost 80 percent during the 1973–1976 period and is still rising.[22]

In response to rising costs, most newspapers raised both advertising and circulation rates. These measures reduced at least temporarily, both linage and circulation, dampening income growth. As a result, the profitability of many newspapers receded. Even where profits rose, the growth of inflation often caused a decline of *real* profits. In other words, a dollar of profit today is worth considerably less in terms of purchasing power than a dollar of profit five or ten years ago. Just as labor needs wage increases to keep abreast of rising prices, business needs profit growth to stay even with inflation.

Fortunately, U.S. newspapers have not had the severe profit problems of their counterparts in Western Europe. However, some analysts question the future of U.S. newspaper profits if inflation rates continue. Others believe that the advance of technology and productivity in the newspaper business will mean higher profits or at least preserve a reasonable level of profit for most U.S. newspapers.

Newspaper companies, public or private, use their profits much like other businesses. Earnings, after taxes and dividends, provide working capital. They may be used to modernize buildings and equipment for efficiency; improve editorial quality; conduct research and development; pay off loans, or acquire additional properties. Any earnings invested in the company to help generate higher profits in the future are called "retained earnings."

There is no formula to determine the amount to be retained or how it should be used. A rapidly growing company needs retained earnings to help finance that growth; a company that is deeply in debt needs retained earnings to reduce that debt; a company that has antiquated facilities needs retained earnings for modernization. Using profits for expansion or acquisition long has intrigued executives—and sparked criticisms of management.

The Trend Toward Public Ownership

While most newspapers are privately owned, a trend toward public ownership began in the mid-1960s.

Public ownership helps avoid major estate-tax problems. By redistributing ownership through public stock sales, family-owned papers can avoid federal estate-tax rates of 77 percent on $10 million or more of market value. Most states also have inheritance taxes. The death of a newspaper's principal owner may force his heirs to sell in order to pay tax bills. And it might not be possible to find a buyer who could and would pay a fair price. Many a small business and farm has met its demise due to death taxes, as the U.S. Senate Select Small Business Committee reported in 1976.[23] By issuing shares and going public, estate-tax problems can be minimized and the family, by holding a large block of voting stock, can maintain control.

Another advantage of going public is the capital generated by the stock sale. This capital can be used for expansion, payment of debts and other purposes.

But there also are disadvantages. For one thing, public ownership may subject a newspaper to pressures from stockholders. Stockholders are happy when profits are good, but may call for a management change when they are not. The owner who has gone public loses some control he or she historically has enjoyed.

Ernest Hynds summarized the public ownership debate this way: "The potential economic values . . . are considerable. Its ultimate impact on newspapers remains uncertain. It could cause reader-owners to be more responsive to the needs of newspapers; or it could produce additional pressures to make money and avoid controversy that might interfere with making money."[24]

Group Ownership

Encouraged by tax considerations and additional profit potential, group ownership of newspapers has grown rapidly. By the end of 1976, 174 groups owned 1038 daily papers, an average of six per group. In 1971, by contrast, groups owned only 879 papers. In 1910, only 62 dailies were owned by the 13 groups.[25]

The growth of group ownership concerns some. Many worry about potential monopoly control of news arising from the concentration of ownership, about the possibility that existing properties may be short-changed in obtaining capital for expansion and improvements, and about the possibility that owners will make money at the expense of quality.

According to one newspaper publisher, a friend of his was made publisher of a medium-sized daily acquired by a newspaper group and "was required to return 40 percent net on sales. That lasted, I believe, only two or three years. Yet I cannot conceive the impossibility of the task or the wretchedness of the product he was forced to deliver."[26]

Group executives see things differently. A midwestern group president, for instance, said, "Surplus earnings from our business are adequate to do all that money can do to improve the quality of current holdings as well as to finance the acquisition of additional businesses. To the extent that these two purposes might compete, we would balance them first to assure that we are meeting the responsibilities to the customers, since that is in the long-run interest of the owners."[27] Otis Chandler has stated, "In the case of *Times Mirror*'s four newspapers, we retain within each newspaper enough earnings to carry on a continual program of improving the quality of the individual newspaper as well as capital expenditures for improving plants and equipment."[28] Alvah H. Chapman Jr., president and chief executive officer of Knight-Ridder, points out that in most cases his company feels retained earnings should be used primarily to improve the quality of current holdings, rather than to purchase other properties. Still, he adds, "If a property becomes available in a growth market and is one which would improve and strengthen the group, we would not be averse to acquisition."[29]

Critics say that concentration of ownership of the communications media, including cross-media combinations, conglomerate arrangements, joint operating agreements and group formations, threatens editorial independence. In their book *America, Inc.*, Morton Mintz, a *Washington Post* reporter, and Jerry S. Cohen, a former chief counsel of the Senate Antitrust and Monopoly Subcommittee, point out: "A democratic society must have a free exchange of ideas, dissent and diversity. It may surive a concentration of manufacturing assets in a few conglomerate corporations but it cannot withstand a similar concentration of communications media."[30]

Nonsense, said John C. Quinn, vice president for news of Gannett Co.: "In 20th century newspaperdom, there is no greater myth than the Great Monopoly Diversity Debate." In Quinn's view debaters overlook the reader whose prime concern "is not who owns the newspaper or under what circumstances."[31] The reader's prime concern, he said, is how well the newspaper does its job in exercising the responsibilities of the free press.

Reese Cleghorn, an editor of the *Charlotte* (N.C.) *Observer,* a Knight-Ridder paper wrote: "The increasing concentration of newspaper ownership is of legitimate concern to the profession and to the public, I think. But until the economic laws of newspapers are reversed, we are likely to see more and more of that. Group ownerships sometimes improve newspapers and sometimes damage them. That depends principally upon the professional integrity and concern of the particular group."[32]

The quality of management is a major determinate of the quality of a newspaper—whether it be locally owned or group owned, privately or publicly held. As for group ownership in general, it has been clearly demonstrated that the acquisition of a company may prompt either improvement or deterioration.[33] The great wave of acquisitions by conglomerate corporations in the late 1960s produced disaster for those conglomerates that bled their existing holdings to provide capital for new acquisitions. The lesson from that experience is that product quality *and* financial integrity are essential to future success.

Acquisitions often have saved failing newspapers. For example, The Milwaukee Journal Company purchased its competitor, *The Milwaukee Sentinel,* when it learned there was no other willing buyer and the newspaper was about to close. Nevertheless, the purchase of an unprofitable newspaper and the infusion of funds by a more solvent competitor in the same community is sometimes criticized. Some critics seem to deplore common ownership more than one-paper towns, even though the commonly owned media may have competing editorial voices.

The Federal Communications Commission and Justice Department antitrust attorneys have investigated media combinations and the effects of common ownership. The Justice Department has taken an increasingly harder line and owners are keeping a close eye on developments. Allen Neuharth, Gannett's president and chief executive officer, told security analysts in 1975 that many of the 800-plus independently owned dailies are acquisition candidates and his company is actively in the market. But he said, Gannett plans its acquisitions carefully to avoid any confrontation with the government. The fact that Gannett had holdings in only 17 of the 50 states means it would be "a long, long time, if ever" before the company and the government would clash over acquisition policy.[34]

Considerable evidence supports the claim of group owners that their primary concern and control centers on efficient *business* management of their media enterprises, not on group editorial control. For example, it is not unusual for individual dailies within a newspaper group to have very diverse editorial philosophies ranging from liberal to conservative and from Republican to Democratic. Two commonly owned newspapers within the same state often support different candidates for state and national offices. On the other hand, management functions, such as the purchasing of newsprint, may be centrally managed without infringing on the freedom of editors.

Conclusion

Profits are essential to any type of modern business enterprise because they are compensation for invested capital and a source of new capital for increased quality and productivity. As George Meany, president of the AFL-CIO once said, "We recognize the right of private capital and private management to receive a fair share of the rewards of production. It is only when profits soar way out of line that we become critical of the profit system."[35]

The public has a special vested interest in the profitability of newspapers and the other media because adequate profitability is essential to editorial excellence and to independence from outside pressures.

The editorial personnel of a newspaper should recognize the importance of profitability and the business activities of their newspaper. However, this recognition and communication with their business associates should never be allowed to infringe upon their basic editorial independence.

NOTES
Chapter 4

[1] The newspaper itself is, of course, a consumer product while advertising services are an industrial product.

[2] Letter to contributing author, August 4, 1975.

[3] From an article in an employe newsletter (also in 1974 annual report).

[4] Ben H. Bagdikian, "Newspaper Economics, So What?," Journalism Newsletter, University of Maryland, Spring 1975, p. 1.

[5] David M. Rubin, " 'Behind the Front Page,' " [MORE], November 1974, an article/review of Behind the Front Page (San Francisco: Jossey-Bass, 1974) by Chris Argyris.

[6] Arthur R. Taylor, "Business and the Media: 'A Lack of Respect,' " Washington Post, December 14, 1975, op-edit page.

[7] John H. Colburn, "Economics of the Press," Proceedings: Education for Newspaper Journalists in the Seventies and Beyond, American Newspaper Publishers Association Foundation in cooperation with the Association for Education in Journalism, October 31, November 1 & 2, 1973, p. 102.

[8] Letter to contributing author, August 1, 1975.

[9] Claude Robinson, Understanding Profits (Princeton, New Jersey: D. Van Norstrand, Inc., 1961), p. 188.

[10] For a fuller discussion see "The Blessings and Evils of Profit" by Jon G. Udell, University of Wisconsin-Madison.

[11] Peter F. Drucker, The Age of Discontinuity, (New York: Harper & Row Publishers, 1969), p. 146.

[12] Speech at an NYSE Conference on Ecouraging International Capital Flows, New York, September 23, 1975.

[13] The New York Stock Exchange, "International Implications of a United States Capital Shortage," Research Department, September 1975, p. iii.

[14] Ibid. p. iv.

[15] Ernest C. Hynds, American Newspapers in the 1970s, (New York: Hastings House, 1975), p. 125.

[16] The 13 companies are: Affiliated Publications, based in Boston, publisher of the Boston Globe; Booth Newspapers, Inc., based in Ann Arbor, Mich., owner of eight dailies in Michigan; Capital Cities Communications, Inc., based in New York, owner of Fairchild Publications and three dailies in three states; Dow Jones & Co., Inc., based in New York, owner of the Wall Street Journal, National Observer, Barron's and a subsidiary that publishes 12 general circulation dailies in six states; Gannett Co., Inc., based in Rochester, N.Y., owner of 73 dailies in 28 states; Harte-Hanks Communications, Inc., based in San Antonio, Texas, owner of 21 dailies in six states; Knight-Ridder Newspapers, Inc., based in Miami, Fla., owner of 35 dailies in 16 states; Lee Enterprises, Inc., based in Davenport, Iowa, owner of 14 dailies in six states; Media General, Inc., based in Richmond, Va., owner of six dailies in three states; Multi-media, Inc., based in Greenville, S.C., owner of eight dailies in four states; the New York Times Co., owner of the New York Times and 13 affiliated dailies in Florida and North Carolina; Speidel Newspapers, Inc. (now a part of Gannett); Times Mirror Co., based in Los Angeles, owner of four dailies including the Los Angeles Times, Newsday on Long Island and the Dallas Times Herald; and the Washington Post Co., based in Washington, D.C., and owner of two dailies in the District of Columbia and Trenton, N.J. (Data based on Annual Reports, 1976).

[17] John Morton Newsper Research Newsletter, Colin Hochstin Co., April 18, 1977.

[18] Calculated from sales and profit statistics reported by the U.S. Department of Commerce, Survey of Current Business, vol. 57, no. 5, May, 1977.

[19] Edward E. Dunleavy, "Newspaper Industry An Overview," Merrill Lynch Pierce Fenner & Smith, April 1975, p. 27.

[20] Letter tc contributing author, August 4, 1975.

[21] Letter to contributing author, August 5, 1975.

[22] For a more detailed discussion of newsprint prices, see Chapter 8, pp. 124–125.

[23] Hearings of the Select Committee on Small Business, U.S. Senate, 1975 and 1976.

²⁴ Hynds, *op. cit.*, p. 138.
²⁵ Raymond B. Nixon, "Trends in U.S. Newspaper Ownership: Concentration with Competition, *Mass Media and Society,* 2d edition, edited by Alan Wells (Mayfield Publishing Company, 1975), p. 14 (reprinted from Gazette, XIV, No. 3, 1968, pp. 181–93, updated).
²⁶ Letter to contributing author.
²⁷ Letter to contributing author.
²⁸ Letter to contributing author.
²⁹ Letter to contributing author.
³⁰ Morton Mintz and Jerry S. Cohen, *America, Inc.* (New York: The Dial Press, 1971), p. 77.
³¹ John C. Quinn, "The Big Myth," Nieman Reports, September 1972, p. 9.
³² "The Monopoly of Opinion," The Masthead, National Conference of Editorial Writers, Fall 1974, p. 19.
³³ Jon G. Udell, "Social and Economic Consequences of the Merger Movement in Wisconsin," U.S. Senate Select Committee on Small Business and Subcommittee on Financial Markets, June 1975, pp. 551–638.
³⁴ "Gannett Plans to Buy More Newspapers," Editor & Publisher, August 30, 1975, p. 22. As of mid-1977, Gannett owned newspapers in 28 states, primarily because of its acquisition of Speidel Newspapers, Inc.
³⁵ Robinson, *Understanding Profits,* p. 9.

5

Quality, Price and Planning

THE SUCCESS of a newspaper depends primarily on its quality, both as a newspaper and as a business enterprise. There are exceptions. Some temporarily successful newspaper organizations do not produce quality newspapers. There have been a few quality products that were not successful—the *New York Herald-Tribune,* for example.

In general though, a successful newspaper is of high quality *and* is well managed and efficiently distributed to its customers. Editorially it has balanced news, interesting features, thoughtful opinion and readable typography. A quality product is usually costly, therefore good management is required to keep costs within reason and to generate the revenues necessary to cover those costs.

Elements of a Quality Newspaper

While a newspaper is a physical product, it provides a service—a communication service to the public. Whether the public considers that service vital depends on reader interest.

Good management can produce an interesting paper that the reader will judge to be of high quality. But quality is not just the product of a good editor who concentrates on creating an interesting newspaper each day. Behind the successful editor is an effective organization, a consistently profitable organization that generates financial resources necessary to provide the ingredients of quality—good people, good equipment and good materials. With those an editor can create an excellent newspaper.

How does the public judge newspaper quality? Is it appearance of the front page—accuracy of news coverage—editorial comment—special features—advertising? Obviously, all of these and more.

A quality newspaper is one that is recognized as such not only by press critics, but most importantly by the readers in a community. They must think enough of a newspaper to buy it regularly. Quality newspapers are profitable; they are not supported by some private interest.

It is the total product that is judged by the consuming public: (1) news content; (2) features; (3) opinion; (4) advertising; (5) physical appearance; (6) delivery service, and (7) community involvement.

News Content

News content is the most important element of a newspaper's quality. But too frequently students complete journalism schools not understanding that news quality requires not only good writing, accuracy and completeness of detail, investigative reporting, and depth of analysis, but also *balance.* The balanced presentation of news is essential to real quality. However, a few unbalanced speciality newspapers are judged as excellent by a minor segment of the population.

A quality community newspaper must have a balance of news content, honest and accurate local news, and significant quantities of well-edited regional, national and international news. There also needs to be a balance of news about the young and old; the poor, the rich and the great middle class; a balance of religion, science, education and art; balance among business, government and labor; humor balanced by pathos; statistics balanced by pictures; and sports balanced by politics. A newspaper's readership spans four generations—ages 8 through 100—and all wish to read a quality newspaper of interest *to them.*

Features

Newspaper features are usually added in proportion to news content to give the reader information that can help him or her live a full life. Some features should be fun, others can be heavy. All need not have universal appeal: Some may have a following of only 3 to 10 percent of all readers, but eliminating them would cause angry reader response.

Features are the mustard, catsup and spice on the meat and potatoes of news. Good writers bring sparkle and charm to features. A profitable newspaper can pay the salaries necessary to keep talented writers. Feature writers with styles that readers enjoy help a newspaper develop loyal readers.

Opinion

Editorial opinions, reader commentaries and analyses of news stories are instrumental in establishing a newspaper's personality. Clearly stated opinions make a newspaper loved or hated by certain community elements. But, if its opinions are basically honest and intelligent, a newspaper will develop trust and respect, and a loyal following.

To maintain a quality image in readers' eyes, a newspaper must be strong and firm. Readers should believe their newspaper cares about the common good over the long term, even though a short run "easy out" may be suggested by others. This requires editorial character backed by financial strength.

Advertising

Advertising is news. Many people buy newspapers to learn what products and services are available, where and at what prices. In addition, a quality newspaper's advertising needs to have character too.

Media are frequently judged by their *advertising* content. This content is especially important to a newspaper which presents its image to the public each day.

Advertising should be honest. The general appearance of ads needs to be pleasant, and its content in keeping with the mores of the community. Statements made by advertisers must be reasonable. Good newspapers police advertising copy in order to preserve its reliability. Requiring *all* advertisers to meet established standards takes character and perseverance. It is difficult for a financially weak newspaper to display such character. A weak newspaper may need every possible line of advertising in order to survive. Fortunately, most U.S. newspapers are not in a "do or die" position.

Physical Appearance

To present a favorable image a newspaper needs to print an *attractive product*. Although newsprint is on the low end of the paper-quality spectrum, a newspaper can be a "clean" product. To be clean is to be relatively error-free and attractive in appearance. Words and pictures should be clear and easily readable. Good printing quality requires good equipment operated by well-trained people.

Profits must be reinvested regularly in the operation to update equipment. Attractive salaries are necessary to retain able employes who can make the most of modern equipment. Good management and sound policies are required to reduce the chance of costly, quality-damaging strikes by labor unions over wages, benefits and working conditions.

Delivery Service

A quality newspaper must be *delivered:* (1) at the appropriate time and place; (2) consistently throughout the year, and (3) in the same condition that it left the newspaper plant. A morning newspaper should be on the doorstep by 6:00 a.m.; an evening newspaper in the home by 4:30 p.m. Careless, unreliable distribution of an otherwise quality newspaper will harm its usefulness to a reader. Editors want their newspapers to have the latest possible news deadlines, but most of them also realize that delivery must be timely if their newspaper is to be thoroughly read and appreciated by the customer.

Community Involvement

The most important judges of a newspaper are not on the college campus or in political capitals, but in private homes. In order to maintain a quality reputation among its readers, a newspaper should be involved in *community affairs.* Local news gathering should be comprehensive and effective. Editorials on community problems should be intelligent and fair. A newspaper should demonstrate a healthy, sincere interest in the success of community, people, industries and institutions. But community enthusiasm should not be so great that a paper becomes blind to community needs and shortcomings.

Pricing a Quality Product

Financial strength and profitability do not automatically ensure a quality newspaper. Obviously, each dimension of newspaper quality must be properly managed. Proper management requires not only talent, but a clear and accurate understanding of the market which the newspaper wishes to serve.

In its broadest sense, the "market" includes not only readers and advertisers, but also competitors and the overall social/economic climate of the community. For example, management makes pricing decisions. These decisions hinge not only on the financial needs of the newspaper and potential reactions of customers, but also the current and potential prices of competitors.

Interestingly, a rise in the price of a competitor's newspaper can have a mixed market reaction. Some readers will switch to the lower-priced paper. However, if a reader subscribes to two newspapers, he or she may drop *either* one of the two, depending upon which is thought to be of most value. For example, *The Milwaukee Journal* experienced a decline in out-of-town circulation when a newspaper in a neighboring locale raised its circulation rates. Apparently, some subscribers believed they could no longer afford both newspapers and continued to subscribe to the local newspaper even though it had increased its price. This phenomenon is one of the factors that has led to the decline of out-of-town circulation of many metropolitan newspapers.

As of 1977 the typical price for a daily newspaper was 15 cents per copy, although prices ranged from 5 to 25 cents, and 20 cents was becoming increasingly common. There is no typical advertising rate because those rates vary directly with circulation. In general, the more readers a newspaper has, the more it can and does charge for a page of advertising.

Obviously, low rates enhance market penetration. But very low rates usually provide too little revenue to cover costs. On the other hand, very high rates can so limit sales that resulting revenue fails to cover operating costs. The goal is to find a profitable balance—rates which will allow a newspaper to develop its market potential, cover the cost of a quality newspaper and yield an adequate return on the capital invested in the enterprise.

Planning and Budgeting

Establishment of reasonable volume goals is a major step in a newspaper's planning and budgeting process.

But before goals can be set, management must assess the strengths, weaknesses, problems and opportunities of both the paper and its market. Some of these factors are beyond management control—the price of newsprint, local retail sales, household growth or unemployment—but they must be taken into account.

Once this assessment is completed, the sales management (advertising sales manager and circulation manager) can project advertising linage and circulation for the planning period—which can vary from three months to five years or more, but normally is one year. Advertising and circulation rates are then applied to the volume forecasts to convert them to projected revenue. That, with current liquid assets, provides an estimate of financial resources available to a newspaper during the planning period. Management, using its best judgment of the economic future of the community, evaluates the revenue forecast and approves it—with or without modification.

The forecasts become budgeted volume goals for circulation, advertising linage and revenue. Other goals are established for costs, productivity (such as man hours per page), percentage of paid space, and market penetration. Often quality goals are also established, such as objectives for personnel development and facility improvement.

For each goal there should be a plan of action. For example, management determines the amount of news and feature content necessary to provide a quality product for the reader. A minimum quantity of news for each day's paper is normally determined jointly by business managers and editors. When advertising volume permits, provision is made for increased news and feature content. Each newspaper typically develops its own standard relationship between news and advertising content. This relationship may differ considerably from one newspaper to another. However, successful newspapers generally have about twice the amount of paid advertising as unpaid space which includes news, features and editorials.

A newspaper's size will determine its raw material costs, principally newsprint and ink. Other production costs, for manpower and supplies, also are influenced by the size and production volume of a newspaper.

As a part of budgeting, management establishes the level of operation of all essential functions of a newspaper. The editor plans the size of his staff and operating expenses for wire and feature services, travel and other necessities. The circulation manager presents an operating plan for future distribution of the newspaper, showing the related costs for retaining and expanding circulation. Managers of advertising, promotion, research and administration likewise submit their plans to management. Their plans include desired staff size, pay levels and necessary expenses including the cost of employe fringe benefits, supplies and taxes.

The financial executive, who has participated as part of the budgeting team, computes an estimated operating statement from the plans submitted and forwards it to management for review. If the plans allow reasonable profit, they are approved. However, frequently the profit objective is not met, and management must meet with each department manager—including the editor—in an attempt to modify planned expenditures for staff and other expenses. One of management's basic functions is to exercise the judgment necessary to adjust each part of the newspaper's operation so as to attain the financial result necessary to keep the newspaper economically strong. This often is not a pleasant task but is a very vital one.

Management insists that the budget be the basic operational plan for the newspaper which should be adhered to under normal circumstances. Variations from budget can be authorized on special request. Departmental managers realize their performance is being monitored against the budget, and that they will be called upon to explain any substantial deviations from it. With this clearly understood and the financial objectives explained to all departmental managers, an atmosphere of cooperation can develop within the newspaper. Those responsible for the quality of a newspaper will realize that bigger budgets—and higher quality—are made possible by adequate profits, and they will work to attain those profits.

Many managers mistakenly equate quality of the product with the amount of money spent on the operation. The theory of some editors, for example, is that a larger budget for more people, additional wire services or more newsprint for a larger news hole automatically means that quality of the product will increase. But, improved quality does not come automatically from more money. Hard work, good organization and intelligent effort are required to obtain improved quality with or without more money being spent. Sometimes improved quality results from a budget reduction. However, this is rarely admitted by a department manager whose budget has been cut. Newspaper quality does not come easily. It requires the efforts and cooperation of a team of good people every day of the year.

Monitoring Performance

Until recently, many newspapers had not developed meaningful measures of performance. Newspaper groups usually have had the most sophisticated measurement systems. However, most newspapers now recognize the importance of timely cost and performance measurements.

These measurements, usually made monthly, compare current costs and revenues to those anticipated in the budget and to those recorded during the same period the previous year. These periodic analyses enable management to scrutinize current revenue, circulation and other performance objectives. Cost and productivity measurements include:

Manhours per news column.
Manhours and cost per column of display and classified advertising.
Productive manhours per page.
Overtime, by department.
Percentage of distribution costs to circulation revenue by zones and type of sale (carriers, newsstands and motor routes).
Tons and cost of newsprint used and newsprint wastes.

The number of cost calculations and ratios—such as cost to budget comparisons—varies by newspaper. Usually a computer is used. The goal of cost measurement is to provide management with timely information needed to identify cost problems and to evaluate the efficiency of all newspaper operations.

Conclusion

Quality in newspaper publishing comes from the combined efforts of an integrated management team. While casual readers tend to equate news coverage and editing with newspaper quality, there are many other elements involved. Among these are features and opinion columns, advertising, physical appearance, delivery service and community involvement.

The financial health of a newspaper is basic to success in all these areas. The editor of a financially sound newspaper is free to resist any pressures from advertisers, special interest groups and politicians.

Quality is best achieved within a framework of long-range planning, budgeting and an understanding of the market being served. Revenue forecasts and budgets are the operational tools by which management controls the growth and development of a newspaper.

6

The Dynamics of Newspaper Production

AMERICAN NEWSPAPERS are undergoing a technological revolution. Twenty years ago newspapers were produced in ways essentially unchanged for half a century. Most of the advances of that previous half century speeded up certain processes, mainly typesetting and press runs, but production techniques were basically unchanged.

In the early 1900s the production processes of daily newspapers were as advanced as those of any other industry. The invention of the hot metal type-setting machine by Ottmar Mergenthaler in 1886, coupled with other nineteenth century inventions, such as the rotary press and stereotype, made the daily newspaper an early example of partial automation. But then a long hiatus in newspaper technological advancement caused the production efficiency of newspapers to fall behind that of other industries.

The Publishers' Decision

First radio and then television arrived to compete with newspapers for both public attention and advertising revenues. Technological advances came rapidly in manufacturing fields from automobiles to home appliances. The computer exploded onto the scene. Communications technology advanced rapidly with development of microwave systems, communications satellites, printed circuits and miniaturization.

Some observers even predicted the newspaper would become an obsolete medium because it was saddled with archaic and expensive production processes which were not competitive. In the early 1960s, electronic technology further enhanced the growth opportunities for television and radio as news, advertising and entertainment media. Color became commonplace in television; communications from networks to broadcast stations became faster and more efficient and television stop-action and replay techniques were developed. It was at this time that the newspaper publishing business made one of its most significant and historic decisions—to adapt new electronic technology to the newspaper production process rather than regard it as competition. That decision has paid handsome dividends.

The Evolutionary Revolution: First—Offset

Historically, newspaper publishers usually have insisted that new technology be applied gradually. Newspapers have large capital investments in existing machinery. New processes not compatible with other steps in the production system require further changes which may eliminate any cost saving.

In many instances labor union contracts contained clauses which made adoption of new processes difficult, or imposed staffing levels which made the new processes uneconomic. In addition, the adoption of new newspaper production technology required reeducation of most newspaper departments.

Small, weekly newspapers often are credited with providing the first major stimulus to the technological revolution in daily newspaper publishing. In the 1950s the weeklies rediscovered an old printing process called offset-lithography in which the page image on a smooth, photosensitive plate is transferred or "offset" to a rubber blanket and thence to the surface of the paper.

Offset uses the principle that oil (ink) and water are mutually repellent. The wetter certain parts of the plate, the less ink will adhere. Offset's disadvantage is that the ink-water balance is critical, and there may be considerable waste of paper at the start of a press run as that critical balance is achieved. Its great advantage is its high-quality picture reproduction which encourages the use of photographs and makes graphic display innovations possible.

Since most weekly newspapers have short press runs, they do not need multiple plates for each page as large dailies do for their several editions. Hence, for weeklies, the amount of wasted paper is not so significant. Thus, the offset process was a natural for hundreds of weekly newspapers, and their publishers rapidly began conversion to the new process. Several manufacturers began to compete for the market with small-capacity, rotary offset presses.

Slowly, small daily newspapers began to investigate the use of offset. For years only one daily newspaper in the United States, the *Opelousas* (La.) *Daily World,* used offset printing. Then, the American Newspaper Publishers Association Research Institute, recognizing the potential for offset in the daily field, began to collect information needed to advise its members on offset's advantages and disadvantages and held several conferences for publishers examining the process and its implications for dailies.

In the early days of conversions to offset, it was thought that the difficulty of making last-minute changes in a page image would make offset impractical for all but morning dailies. Afternoon dailies were thought to be on too tight deadline and production schedules. This problem was solved, and afternoon dailies joined the parade to offset.

It was also once thought that only the smaller dailies could economically convert to offset because of newsprint waste and other problems of longer press runs. Conventional wisdom at one time said that 35,000 daily circulation was the upper limit for offset. But publishers soon found that no formula could predict successful conversion to offset; the factors of each individual case had to be examined carefully. Those factors included total circulation, distribution patterns, volume of news composition, volume of display and classified advertising, peak volume in number of pages, news deadlines, patterns of competing media and the current status of investments and technology of the newspaper.

Offset worked. And other dramatic changes were in the wind as well.

The Newspaper Production Process—Old and New

Regardless of the technology involved, newspaper production involves collection and assembly of news and advertising into pages, printing and folding, and distribution to readers. Figure 1 shows the flow of this process and provides a basis for the following discussion of the dynamic changes that have made the newspaper a modern medium of communication and assured it a bright future.

The Traditional Letterpress System

The two great weaknesses of the traditional, metal-based production system are the need for multiple keyboarding of copy—typewriter and

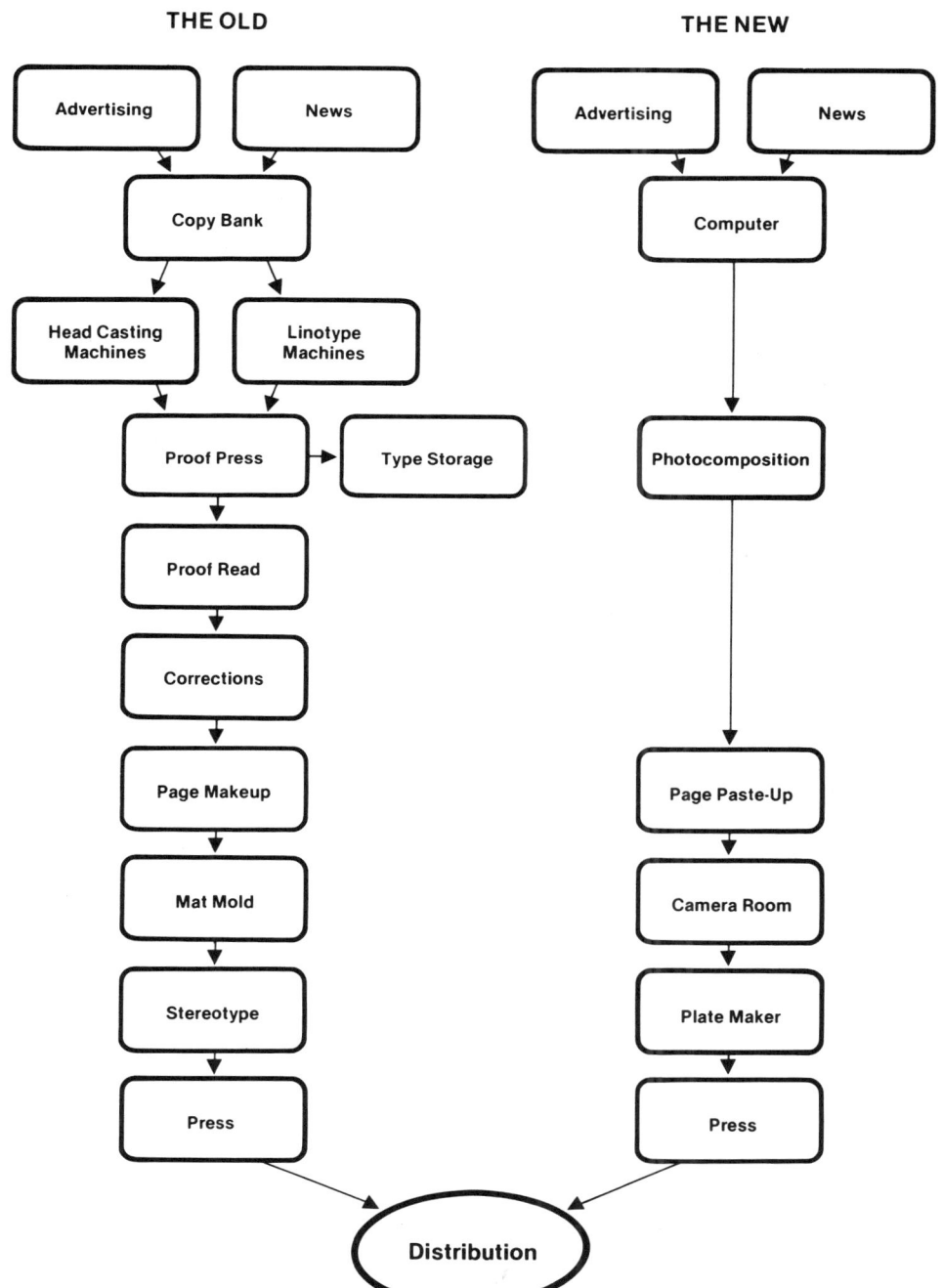

Figure 1
PRODUCING A NEWSPAPER

linecaster—and multiple conversions between positive and negative images—photo development and engraving, and stereotyping.

The term "hard copy" is used to describe news and advertising in typed or written form. Under the old system, all original material was in the form of hard copy. Reporters typed stories on paper, and editors edited them with soft pencils, eventually sending them to the composing room with many markings which typesetting machine operators had to follow in re-keyboarding the news stories.

Wire service news stories also came in the form of hard copy on teletypewriters. Mimeographed feature material often came through the mail. Obviously, all such material had already been typed or "keyboarded" at least once at its source but had to be re-keyboarded again by printers on type-setting machines at each newspaper.

Display advertising came to the newspaper in every imaginable form—from final plates or mats to layouts and copy scribbled on the back of an envelope. Advertising copy often had to be retyped at the newspaper before printers could keyboard it again on typesetting machines.

Some classified advertising also came in a variety of typed or handwritten copy, but for most newspapers a high percentage of classified advertising was taken by telephone. Even for relatively small amounts of revenue, many separate steps were necessary to prepare classified advertising copy for the composing room, to verify the credit standing of the customer, to place the ad in its proper section of the classified pages, and to prepare the bill.

Each news story, feature item and advertisement—both display and classified—was sent to the composing room as a separate item, marked up under a system of hieroglyphics which told the typesetters what sizes of type, line lengths and special effects were to be used. Even headlines for news stories had to be written on separate pieces of paper because they were not set on the same machines as the news stories themselves.

Display advertising could become extremely complex with mixtures of plain typesetting, called "straight matter," photographs and line drawings. Some advertisers liked parts of their ads set on a diagonal, or "mortised" into a portion of a picture or a drawing. The more complex the layout the slower and more expensive the composition process.

Each item of news and advertising was produced in *metal* slugs from the hot-metal (molten lead) typesetting machines in the composing room. These metal items were then inked and proofs were printed by hand on small proof presses. The next step was proofreading to correct all errors which had been made in the re-keyboarding typesetting process. A major weakness of this old system was that any error, no matter how small, required resetting at least one full line on the typesetting machine. This in turn introduced the possibility of new errors on the "corrected" line.

After proofreading, each page had to be assembled in a metal frame called a "chase" on a rolling table called a "turtle." This was a cumbersome process involving the ever-present possibility of dropping type, thus mixing up all the separate lines or "slugs" into a mess called "pi." In such cases there was often nothing to do but re-set the entire item.

When advertisements or stories included photographs, photoengraved half-tones—usually on zinc or magnesium but later in plastic— had to be made. Often engraving was a bottleneck in the process, especially in the case of late news or advertising copy.

When the metal page pieces finally were assembled in the composing room, the turtle was rolled to the stereotyping department where a papier mâché mat was pressed heavily against the made-up page. The mat, with its mirror image of the page was then used to produce semi-cylindrical metal plates. Molten lead was poured on the mat, now curved, in a big, heavy stereotype machine. Since each page plate weighed about 40 pounds, it had to be moved to the press by some kind of conveyor system.

The rotary press, running multiple stereotype plates to produce newspapers of 96 or more pages, was an early production marvel. It is still a highly efficient machine; however, a piece of machinery as heavy as a locomotive is being used to transfer ink to paper.

At the end of the press itself is the folder which converts an enormous amount of printed matter into neatly folded daily newspapers. These are moved, usually on a roller conveyor system, to a "mail room" where bundles of newspapers are counted, tied and labeled if necessary for dealers or mail subscribers and placed in trucks for delivery to neighborhood carriers.

The New System

From the first to the last steps in the process, the new system takes advantage of the computer and of new communications technology to store original keystrokes and to eliminate multiple keyboarding of copy. It also reduces the number of conversions between positive and negative images, or automatically makes conversions.

At the beginning of the process are the reporter's keystrokes when he or she types a news story. Reporters' electric typewriters, or terminals, are tied to electronic devices in the new system which "store" each keystroke. Here's how it works:

From the electric typewriter comes copy which can be edited and composed through two different processes without the necessity of re-keyboarding. One is through the Optical Character Reader (OCR), a device which can "sense" typewritten copy if it is prepared in a compatible typeface. The OCR converts the copy to electronic or taped signals which activate a photocomposing machine to produce "cold type" in film or paper form.[1] The reporter's hard copy can be edited with a felt pen, the markings from which are invisible to the OCR's scanner. A typist then inserts final editing changes by typing between the lines with an electric typewriter like the original. The OCR then produces cold type from the edited version.

The other system involves production of the original news story without any hard copy at all. The reporter types on an electric keyboard which is part of a device called a Cathode Ray Tube (CRT) or Video Display Terminal (VDT) because a screen similar to a television set is connected to the keyboard. The reporter can read what he or she has written and can change it on the keyboard and screen as often as wished. When finally satisfied with a story, the reporter simply informs the appropriate editor who can "call up" the story from the computer onto his own VDT screen and edit it as necessary. When all editing is completed, the story remains in electronic storage to be called up whenever wanted for virtually instantaneous electronic typesetting.

Wire services were in the vanguard of this new technology. They had long been transmitting news in a form which could be fed automatically into teletypesetters—automatic, hot-metal, typesetting machines actuated by punched paper tape. Today all wire-service copy is transmitted in forms which are compatible with VDT systems used by newspapers, thus eliminating the necessity for re-keyboarding. Also, columns and other feature material are made available in a variety of forms including OCR or camera-ready copy for immediate integration into a page image for the press.

As in the old system, elements of the newspaper content—news, features and advertising—are assembled into pages. This is done today mainly by "pasting up" the photoset elements into page images. However, this process also can be done on film, and the whole assembly operation can even be done automatically within a computer. If a VDT screen is large enough on which to assemble a full page, and if the computer capacity is great enough, the page image can go from VDT via computer to platemaking.

As more and more newspapers adopted the offset printing method, the costly and time-consuming platemaking process attracted competitive attention from manufacturers. Furthermore, photocomposition became so economical and reliable that even letterpress newspapers also began using it. Several manufacturers soon developed shallow-relief, plastic plates to replace metal plates. Other manufacturers developed systems which produced "pattern" plates that could be used for stereotyping. The ANPA Research Institute developed a unique combination of the letterpress and offset systems, known as Di-Litho TM, under which an offset type of plate could be used on letterpress units.

As all this new technology developed, it was integrated gradually into the newspaper production system. Each development led to another potential bottleneck as the system changed. The early conversions to offset printing stimulated photocomposition advances. Photocomposition in turn made better page imaging necessary. Next plastic press plates came into use. Now the press itself is the target for improvement. Lighter weight rotary presses are being sought. Researchers even have demonstrated early versions of plateless printing using ink jets or other systems by which a computer is used to transfer page images to the paper running through a plateless "press."

Most newspaper readers and many newspaper employes take production of the daily newspaper for granted. However, if radio and television had been invented first, the newspaper surely would be regarded as a modern miracle.

Unlike other manufacturers, a publisher starts each day not knowing what his or her final product will look like, what will be its ingredients and, often, how many will be produced. The product has a retail shelf-life of less than 24 hours. It is not stockpiled for future sale. It must be delivered to the customer more quickly than almost any other product. And, amazingly, it is sold to the consumer for less than it costs to manufacture, and is delivered to one home at a time. Each newspaper still costs most subscribers about the price of one first-class postage stamp.

Only by vigorously adopting even more advanced technological developments can the newspaper business continue its miraculous feats throughout the rest of the 20th century. The potential impact of advancing technology on the newspaper of the near future is discussed in Chapter 10.

Capital Requirements of the Modern Newspaper

Just how much capital investment is required to convert to the new technology depends on a newspaper's size and the extent of new systems adopted. In general, the capital investment required for the new technology usually compares favorably with the costs of replacing traditional newspaper equipment.

Cost and sophistication of photocomposing equipment vary greatly. Photocomposers are available for a few thousand dollars—or for upwards of $200,000. If a publisher wants to reduce substantially the number of people needed in the composing room, his capital outlay will be higher than if his primary goal simply is to take advantage of the speed and flexibility of photocomposition.

Whatever the primary goal of converting to photocomposition, two facts stand out: Efficiency and flexibility are markedly higher with cold type than with hot type processes; and total capital investment is considerably lower for cold type than for hot-type machinery of equivalent production capacity. Because a photocomposing machine operates at many times the speed of a metal linecasting machine, one photocomposing machine can replace several of the older machines.

The last year (1968) new hot metal linecasting machines were available for purchase, each cost about $25,000 in basic form. Even a relatively unsophisticated, $50,000-plus photocomposition system can do the work of 10 linecasting machines.

Thus a small newspaper with 10 hot-metal machines had a capital investment of $250,000 in linecasting machines alone. That newspaper could convert to photocomposition, retaining about the same size labor force, for $50,000 to $62,500. For another $50,000, that same newspaper could buy a scanner (Optical Character Reader) and electric typewriters instead of using papertape perforators to activate the photocomposer, thereby significantly reducing the payroll in the composing room. For an additional $20,000, the paper could buy a video terminal to handle all of its classified ads without any typewriters.

A larger-circulation newspaper with 40 to 50 linecasting machines, representing a replacement value of more than $1 million, could convert its composing room to a sophisticated system with photocomposers, scanners, VDT terminals and a computer for perhaps $500,000. And that investment would permit a considerably reduced payroll in the composing room.

Offset presses are not dramatically cheaper than letterpresses with comparable capacities, speed and quality. Like letterpresses, offset presses vary tremendously in price. A 10,000-circulation newspaper with an average of 16 pages a day probably would spend $130,000 for a new offset press, including installation. A newspaper with 100,000 circulation and an average of 48 pages probably would need $3,500,000 or more for installed presses. For circulations greater than 100,000 and page capacities of more than 48, prices are extremely difficult to predict. The *St. Louis Post-Dispatch,* with a circulation of just over 300,000, spent $12 million for new offset presses a few years ago. Prices have risen considerably since that time.

If the letterpress process is retained, conversion to photocomposition requires purchase of shallow-relief platemaking equipment. It costs $25,000 to $100,000 depending upon capacity. If a newspaper converts to the offset process, equivalent outlays are needed for offset platemaking equipment.

Thus, a small daily newspaper with a 10,000 circulation and 16 pages a day can convert entirely to the new technology in printing, news and advertising departments for about what was previously necessary for hot-metal composing equipment alone. This capital investment would include new photocomposition equipment, scanner, VDT editing and classified terminals, a computer and electric typewriters for the newsroom and advertising departments. Similar, though not so dramatic, capital advantages accrue to larger newspapers as well.

Many publishers, concerned about possible electronic failures and servicing for modern equipment, prefer to spend more than the minimum capital required in order to provide "backup" capacity. Probably the most common backup machinery is photocomposing equipment, although backup scanners are also common. The more backup capacity ordered, the more modernization costs.

Some newspapers which have purchased backup equipment use the extra equipment to do contract work, much like a commercial printer. Weekly newspapers traditionally have earned substantial revenues—sometimes half of their total—from contract printing. Larger dailies historically have not engaged in such activities, but revenues earned from selling excess composer, scanner or press time can be substantial and help defray capital costs.

One financial advantage of converting to the new technology is not so apparent. The traditional hot-metal, letterpress newspaper operation was captive to its capital investment in equipment. That investment could be "recovered" through amortization, to be sure. But Internal Revenue Service rules require that in order to depreciate equipment rapidly for tax purposes, a newspaper must replace the equipment just as rapidly. Before the advent of the new technology, there was little incentive to do either—depreciate or replace rapidly. Unamortized equipment deterred replacement during its tax life. Even after equipment was fully depreciated, in tax terms, the absence of significantly better equipment delayed replacement. In other words, there was no reason to replace old equipment with new, so long as the old worked and the new was only a shiny version of the old.

The new technology has changed all that. For one thing, capital replacement costs are now lower, function for function. This makes capital investment both more attractive and more possible. The new technology provides greater efficiency and flexibility, potential for a reduced payroll *and* a tax writeoff.

The very rapidity of change in technology is also a force for more change. With the new technology, rapid tax writeoff is encouraged because of the continuing development of equipment. Whereas a 20-year life span and "straight line" depreciation were common for newspaper capital investments in the past, writeoff periods of five or even three years are possible today. With a 20-year life and straight-line depreciation, only 5 percent of capital investment could be depreciated for tax purposes in each tax year. With a 5-year life and accelerated depreciation, about one-third of capital investment can be declared in the first year. The more rapidly a newspaper replaces equipment, the greater the tax advantage. Some managers prefer to lease rather than buy equipment as the entire lease cost is tax deductible as a business expense.

All capital outlay figures mentioned here may fluctuate—up in the face of continued inflation, down in the face of intense competition among suppliers of new equipment and software. Just as no formula has been devised to tell a publisher which new processes to adopt, there is no rule of thumb on capital outlay decisions. Each publisher must carefully analyze production and distribution requirements in light of his or her major objectives.

Conclusion

Newspapers were latecomers to the modern technological revolution. While stunning advances were being made in computers and electronic data processing and transmission, newspaper publishers stayed with such time-tested production methods as hot-metal typesetting, the rotary press and the stereotype process.

In the early 1960s, publishers sought ways to apply new technology. In recent years, many newspapers have converted to offset printing, photocomposition and computer technology. And use of Optical Character Readers and Video Display Terminals is replacing the old drudgery of copy preparation.

The introduction of modern technology has raised newspaper productivity and, in many cases, reduced capital investment requirements, particularly for small papers. Such technological advances help to assure that newspapers will remain competitive with other communication media in the years ahead.

NOTES
Chapter 6

[1] "Cold type" is used as a descriptive phase in the newspaper business because "hot" molten lead is not used in this process; instead print images of copy and illustrations are produced and copied photographically on paper.

7

Anatomy of Newspaper Revenues

ADVERTISING is the major source of revenue for the typical American newspaper. Sixty-five to 70 percent of all newspaper revenue originates from advertising. At one time circulation was the major source of revenue, but with the marketing revolution which started in the late 1800s and blossomed in the 1920s, advertising came to the fore.

In recent years some publishers have attempted to recover from the subscriber more of the higher cost of preparing, printing and delivering a newspaper. This trend may continue, particularly with increasing competition from television and radio for the local advertiser's dollar.

A relatively minor share of the typical newspaper's total revenue comes from the sale of sundry services or products. But, for a small daily or weekly newspaper, job printing can be a significant part of total operations, particularly if the newspaper has offset presses adaptable to commercial job work. Some newspapers charge advertisers for production services such as copywriting and layout, research, composition, photography, art work, engravings or film positives, rather than include these services in the basic advertising rate structure. Under such circumstances, sundry revenue often reaches 1 to 5 percent of the total.

Other newspaper revenues sometimes include subscriber insurance premiums for travel and accident insurance, money from the sale of booklets, reprints of newspaper stories, magazine subscriptions, maps and other merchandise. Sale of waste newsprint and scrap paper may be considered either sundry revenue or a reduction in operating cost. Newspaper-sponsored entertainment or educational events may also produce some revenue, although net proceeds usually are given to charity.

Circulation Revenue

"Circulation revenue" includes all proceeds from the sale of the newspaper to the consumer. A newspaper usually receives only a portion of the total price paid by a reader.

Widely divergent systems are used to distribute newspapers, including:
- The "little merchant plan" with carriers and other distributors serving as individual entrepreneurs coordinated by salaried or commissioned district managers employed by the newspaper.
- The little merchant plan with *independent* distributors or contractors managing the "little merchants." Newspapers are sold to the distributors rather than to the "little merchants."
- Agency operations with distributors handling all area newspapers, frequently using one carrier to deliver competing papers.
- Employe delivery with adult employes delivering newspapers.

Except when using employe delivery, a newspaper sells papers to distributors of one type or another at wholesale prices. Sales by mail, employe carriers and newspaper-owned vending machines or other direct sales to customers are at full retail price.

A typical newspaper receives about 70 to 75 percent of the single-copy or home-delivered price as revenue. The relationship of circulation revenue per copy to the retail price of a newspaper will depend on the nature of the paper's sales distribution mix. A newspaper sold principally by mail receives a higher precentage of the retail price as circulation revenue. The same is true of newspapers delivered by employes. However, in both mail and employe delivery, a newspaper incurs the total distribution expense. With the rising cost of postage, labor and gasoline, direct distribution by a newspaper can yield a lower net return (circulation revenue less delivery costs) than other methods of distribution.

Deliveries by school-age carriers, who operate as "little merchants" with their own businesses, yield a somewhat higher return than do newspapers sold through distributors who arrange for final delivery. Sales of newspapers to dealers—stores, hotels, newsstands—generally produce greater wholesale revenue than sales to carriers or distributors. Vending-box sales yield as much as 80 to 90 percent of the single-copy price depending on vending-box type and the honesty of customers and distribution employes. However, if vending boxes are handled by distributors, the return is considerably less because of their wholesale discount. Mail subscription rates can yield the highest revenue per copy if the charge to the customer is the circulation rate plus second-class postage—which is steadily increasing.

Independent Distributors

At one time many metropolitan newspapers used independent distributors. Although the distributors reduced circulation revenue, it also reduced circulation costs because most distribution activities were performed by persons outside the newspaper.

While this arrangement still works for some newspapers, it has caused problems for others. By using any independent distributor, a newspaper loses some control over circulation and revenue. If an independent distributor is not aggressive or does not provide good customer service, circulation and revenue are lost. In some cases, independent distributors charge subscribers a premium price above the list price of the newspaper. This tends to create ill will and circulation losses for a newspaper, even though it vigorously opposes the increased price.

Objectionable practices of some independent distributors have led to law suits against them and to a trend among newspapers to regain control over distribution. This and rising postal costs have increased use of distribution by newspaper employes. However, "little merchants," coordinated by the newspaper rather than an independent contractor, remain the most popular delivery system.

Circulation Revenue Trends

The frequency of collection from the wholesaler or the consumer affects the average rate per copy a newspaper nets from its sales. A single-copy sale is basically a full-price, cash sale, while weekly, monthly or annual customer billings usually are discounted. Prepaid subscriptions for carrier delivery—where the newspaper bills customers directly rather than having carriers collect—have been increasing in recent years. Billings are usually for at least a month and frequently for three months, six months or a year. Credit-card charging also has been increasing throughout the industry and, like prepaid subscriptions, is partially to prevent carrier robberies in metropolitan areas. Changes in payment habits and living patterns, with many family members away from home in the evening, also tend to encourage mail and credit-card collections. These collection methods often include incentive discounts from the single-copy price for subscribers and thus result in lower revenue per copy.

Pricing Practices

Newspapers that operate both morning and evening editions sometimes encourage customers to buy both by offering a "combination" discount rate. Newspapers also frequently have low-cost introductory rates, premium gifts for new orders or incentives for employes to secure new subscriptions. These sales methods also lower net revenue per copy.

Except in the largest metro markets, most daily newspaper circulation is home-delivered. This circulation generally has been considered by advertisers to be the most valuable because of its consistency. Therefore, for many years, newspapers have encouraged home delivery by setting weekly home-delivered rates lower than the single-copy price. Increasing costs of delivering a newspaper to a home have caused some newspapers to eliminate these discounts in recent years. In fact, a few newspapers have gone to a premium charge for home delivery, particularly on sparsely settled motor routes far from the newspaper plant.

Soaring distribution costs and newsprint price increases have forced newspapers to raise circulation rates significantly since 1967. Distribution costs of large-circulation newspapers consist largely of wage-related items and transportation expenses. The effect of inflation on these costs is well known.

After a close examination of circulation revenues compared to distribution costs, some papers have stopped serving geographic areas where distribution cost exceeded circulation revenue and advertisers could not benefit from the readership involved.

Small dailies and weeklies have not felt much pressure to eliminate remote and costly circulation. Their circulation is primarily local, and their newsprint cost is not so great as that of larger newspapers. In addition, there is usually less competitive pressure in small cities, making it somewhat easier to pass on cost increases by raising circulation prices without a substantial loss of circulation. In fact, when a small-city newspaper increases its circulation rates, subscribers often reduce their purchases of large-city newspapers circulating in the community, rather than give up their local newspaper.

Circulation Trends

Faster news-wire services and lower production costs due to technological changes have allowed small-city newspapers to add to their edi-

Table 1
CHANGES IN CIRCULATION IN CITIES OF VARIOUS SIZES
1965–1975

DAILY CIRCULATION

City Size	1965	1975	Change	Percent Change
Less than 100,000	21,868,083	24,586,869	2,718,786	12.4
100,000 to 250,000	7,818,939	7,588,126	− 230,813	− 3.0
250,000 to 500,000	8,020,100	7,476,687	− 543,413	− 6.8
500,000 to 1 million	10,402,542	9,418,935	− 983,607	− 9.5
1 million and over	11,303,963	9,416,713	−1,887,250	−14.4
All U.S. Dailies	59,413,627	58,487,330	− 926,297	− 1.6

SUNDAY CIRCULATION

City Size	1965	1975	Change	Percent Change
Less than 100,000	9,829,122	14,067,221	4,238,099	43.1
100,000 to 250,000	6,862,684	7,304,241	441,557	6.4
250,000 to 500,000	7,721,346	8,050,564	329,218	4.3
500,000 to 1 million	10,005,599	9,492,162	− 513,437	− 5.1
1 million and over	13,800,593	11,675,223	−2,125,370	−15.4
All U.S. Dailies	48,219,344	50,589,411	2,370,067	4.9

Source: Jon G. Udell, U.S. *Economic Growth and Newsprint Consumption* American Newspaper Publishers Association (January, 1977).

torial content and otherwise improve their quality. This, plus the rapid growth of many small cities and suburban areas, has given newspapers in these areas substantial circulation growth. The differing trends between small- and large-newspapers are shown in Table 1.

In general, circulation changes have varied inversely with the size of city. In other words, small towns and cities have enjoyed a considerable growth of circulation, while large cities often have experienced declining circulation. However, much of total circulation lost in large cities is the result of the demise of several large-city newspapers. As shown in Table 2, surviving newspapers in some markets (New York, Boston, Washington, D.C., and Newark) now have stronger circulation-revenue bases. Although total daily circulation of five major cities declined 22 percent in the 1965–1975 period (see Table 2), daily circulation of the *surviving* newspapers rose almost 9 percent.

Effect of Prices on Circulation

In attempting to explain a gradual decline in average circulation per household in recent years, many observers have blamed circulation-rate

Table 2

DAILY CIRCULATION IN FIVE MAJOR CITIES

	1965	1975	Change	% Change
New York Newspapers				
3 Defunct	1,267,679	-0-	−1,267,679	−100.0%
3 Presently Operating	3,165,441	3,421,518	+ 256,077	+ 8.1
Total	4,433,120	3,421,518	−1,011,602	− 22.8%
Chicago Newspapers				
1 Defunct	434,156	-0-	− 434,156	−100.0%
3 Presently Operating	1,860,145	1,778,507	− 81,638	− 4.4
Total	2,294,301	1,778,507	− 515,794	− 22.5%
Boston Newspapers *				
1 Defunct	411,789	-0-	− 411,789	−100.0%
2 Presently Operating	693,584	814,132	+ 120,548	+ 17.4
Total	1,105,373	814,132	− 291,241	− 26.4%
Washington, D.C. Newspapers				
1 Defunct	216,317	-0-	− 216,317	−100.0%
2 Presently Operating	752,789	905,976	+ 153,187	+ 20.4
Total	969,106	905,976	− 63,130	− 6.5%
Newark, N.J. Newspapers				
1 Defunct	280,420	-0-	− 280,420	−100.0%
1 Presently Operating	233,442	364,697	+ 131,225	+ 56.2
Total	513,862	364,697	− 149,165	− 29.0%

Summary of Five Major Cities

	1965	1975	Change	% Change
Defunct Newspapers				
5 Evenings	1,891,703	-0-	−1,891,703	−100.0%
2 Morning	718,658	-0-	− 718,658	−100.0
Total Defunct	2,610,361	-0-	−2,610,361	−100.0%
Presently Operating				
4 Evenings	1,440,357	1,717,524	+ 277,167	+ 19.2%
5 Morning	4,042,528	4,306,453	+ 263,925	+ 6.5
2 All Day	1,222,516	1,260,853	+ 38,337	+ 3.1
Total Operating	6,705,401	7,284,830	+ 579,429	+ 8.6%
Grand Total	9,315,762	7,284,830	−2,030,932	− 21.8%

*Christian Science Monitor excluded.
Source: Audit Bureau of Circulations.

hikes. Circulation rates did not increase much during the 1950s when television was having its greatest impact on the American scene, or during the 1960s as television news came of age. As shown in Table 3, circulation rose during both decades.

Table 3

CIRCULATION GROWTH DURING THE 'FIFTIES AND 'SIXTIES

	Daily Circulation	Sunday Circulation
1950	53,829,072	46,582,348
1960	58,881,746	47,698,651
Increase	5,052,674	1,116,303
% Increase	9.4%	2.4%
1960	58,881,746	47,698,651
1970	62,187,527	49,216,602
Increase	3,225,781	1,517,951
% Increase	5.2%	3.1%

Source: Newspaper Advertising Bureau, Inc.

Although circulation did not grow as fast as population or the number of households, circulators explained that population growth was among the young and the old, and that the resulting gains in the number of households were primarily single-person units and low-income families. These types of households have never been strong newspaper customers. In retrospect, some circulators believe they were negligent in not finding better ways to sell to the young, old and apartment dwellers.

However, let us consider the effects of prices on newspaper sales. The annual newspaper price increase was modest during the 1960s and early 1970s. As shown in Table 4, revenues per unit of daily circulation rose only 4.7 percent during the 1964–1973 period.

In 1973, prices started skyrocketing. There were several causes. Fed-

Table 4

ANNUAL REVENUES PER UNIT OF CIRCULATION

	Daily Circulation	Sunday Circulation
1964	$24.60	$10.27
1973	34.96	16.07
Increase	10.36	5.80
% Increase	42.1 %	56.5 %
% Annual Average Increase	4.7 %	6.3 %

eral price controls from 1971 to 1974 prevented some price increases even though costs were rising. By 1974, costs were rising so rapidly, that many newspapers altered traditional pricing politics. Home-delivery discounts were discontinued and the daily, single-copy price jumped from 10¢ to 15¢ or even to 20¢ or 25¢. Sunday newspaper prices increased correspondingly. As shown in Table 5 revenue from an average unit of daily circulation rose 31.4 percent in just two years.

Table 5

	Revenues Per Unit of Daily Circulation	*Revenues Per Unit of Sunday Circulation*
1973	$34.96	$16.07
1975	45.95	20.39
Increase	10.99	4.32
% Increase	31.4 %	26.9 %
% Annual Average Increase	15.7 %	13.4 %

Source: Newspaper Advertising Bureau, Inc.; 1975 Est. Smith Barney Research Report, May 27, 1975.

These price increases caused some circulation losses, usually of 2 to 5 percent. In multi-newspaper markets, consumers strongly resisted paying 15¢ daily. "Fringe" consumers either quit subscribing or were dropped by newspapers. Daily circulation declined 2.5 million or 4.0 percent and Sunday circulation decreased 600,000 or 1.2 percent between 1973 and 1975.

Because the loss of circulation usually was greatest in multi-newspaper markets, many erroneously concluded that newspaper demand is less "elastic" in so-called "non-competitive markets." However, when circulation rates are raised, some two-paper households stop one paper, especially during a period of rapid inflation. Even if newspapers had not raised subscription rates, the combination inflation and recession would have produced some reduction in the number of two-paper households. While one might think that the daily newspaper is too inexpensive to be affected by general economic trends, the fact is that American consumers spend over $3 billion annually for daily newspapers. Any expenditure of this magnitude is affected by economic developments.

Improvement in television news coverage also has influenced circulation sales. Some experts believe television has prevented some young people from developing newspaper-reading habits. Other analysts believe television whets the reading appetites of the public for more detailed news about today's events.

Current Problems and Opportunities

Newspaper circulation revenues may lag behind the economy in future years unless the business can solve some current problems. Harold Schwartz, vice-president and circulation manager of *The Milwaukee Journal/Sentinel,* outlined the challenges in a 1974 speech at Marquette University College of Journalism:

• *Youth readership.* "Young people from ages 18 to 28 are not purchasing newspapers to the same extent as the older generation. We have a continuing challenge to write and edit newspapers that will meet the needs of each new generation."

• *Reaching minorities.* "I don't believe that we know how to edit a newspaper that the blacks and Chicanos will read without turning off the great majority of our readers who are middle-class whites."

• *Deteriorating household coverage.* "Here in America a number of years ago we sold an average of 1.3 newspapers each day for every family. Today, the average is down to .9 copies per family. Much of this has been the result of a decline of multiple readership of newspapers, with the typical family reading just a single newspaper."

• *Apartment house dweller.* "He is more mobile, has fewer roots in the community, less interest in the area in which he lives, is more difficult to service because of apartment house security and, at the same time, represents a growing segment of the population of our cities."

Resolution of these sorts of problems would improve a newspaper's chances for above-average growth. While some of the problems will be difficult to solve, certain trends do favor newspapers. For example, newspapers have never sold well to 18- to 28-year-old readers, but the current population trend is toward a decrease in the proportion of the population in this age group. Looking ahead, the largest growth of population will be in the over-28 group. Minorities are becoming better educated. As more minorities read better, improve their living standards and become more integrated into their communities, they may well become more active newspaper readers. An unanswered question is the extent to which minorities may demand their own special-interest, ethnic and foreign-language newspapers.

Prior to the 1950s, readership of more than one newspaper each day by many families probably occurred because of (1) substantial use of mass transportation; (2) fewer pages per newspaper than today; (3) low cost per copy; (4) substantial leisure time, and (5) low postal rates which encouraged purchase of out-of-town newspapers. Today's typical reader often does not have time to read two or more papers each day, and high postal rates discourage circulation. Therefore, extensive multiple-newspaper readership may never happen again.

As for the future, without high rates of inflation and/or newsprint shortages, newspaper circulation revenues should grow at approximately the same rate as the gross national product. Circulation revenue undoubtedly will remain the most stable and reliable part of a newspaper's total revenue.

Advertising Revenue

Advertising revenue makes the big difference between success and failure of a newspaper. The nature of a newspaper's advertising revenue depends upon its market, circulation success, past pricing policies, aggressiveness in selling and media competition.

Revenue Related to Market

Newspaper advertising expenditures usually have waxed and waned with the gross national product, personal consumption expenditures and, particularly, with retail sales (see Table 6). However, both total advertising and newspaper advertising have, in several recent years, tended to decline as a percentage of the economy (a major exception was the rapid growth of newspaper advertising in 1976).

Retail sales in an individual market are a useful indicator of what total advertising dollars might be available to media in that market. If a

Table 6

NEWSPAPER ADVERTISING EXPENDITURES AS PERCENT OF:

	Gross National Product	Personal Consumption Expenditures	Retail Sales
1947	0.64	0.92	1.20
1952	0.71	1.14	1.52
1957	0.74	1.16	1.63
1962	0.65	1.03	1.55
1967	0.62	1.00	1.57
1972	0.61	0.96	1.56
1973	0.59	0.94	1.51
1974	0.57	0.91	1.49
1975	0.56	0.87	1.44
1976	0.60	0.95	1.57

Source: McCann Erickson, Inc., U.S. Department of Commerce.

newspaper is well run, it attracts a significant share of the advertising dollars available in its market. Nationally, newspapers receive about 30 percent of all advertising expenditures.

Cities and/or regions vary greatly as retail markets. Population is obviously the major factor, but personal income has a great impact on retail sales per capita. In addition, some cities have better shopping facilities than others, and consumers normally are willing to travel to such better facilities at the expense of communities with lesser ones. If a market has no competition for many miles, all nearby residents must trade in that market. Certain markets are located where people live but do not work, other markets are the opposite; and the retail sales and advertising potential of the areas differ accordingly.

Advertising Revenue and Circulation

A newspaper's advertising success is closely related to its circulation. For advertising to be effective in a newspaper, it must be seen and read by a sufficient number to make it "cost effective." The largest-circulation newspaper in a given market generally gets a disproportionately large amount of newspaper advertising revenue in that market. A competitive second paper, while it may be behind only slightly in circulation, is often a more distant second in advertising revenue.

Revenue and Management Policies

Advertising rates also determine whether a newspaper's advertising linage is relatively large or small in relation to its market. Total revenue obtained under either low or high rates may not be significantly different. But a low-rate newspaper will sell more advertising linage to an advertiser than a high-rate paper because of the relatively fixed ratio of advertising expenditures to retail sales. Also, a newspaper's advertising rates almost always affect its success against competing media, with a low-rate policy attracting business away from competitors.

Some newspapers have highly trained, effectively motivated sales personnel who tap the full potential of their markets. Others may take only what orders come in the front door and allow some business they might attract to go to other media.

A newspaper, with its heavy fixed costs, can achieve a tremendous increase in profits through even a slight increase in ad volume. For example, a newspaper which has newsprint and ink costs of only 20 percent of its total operating cost probably will find that incremental ads sold over and above the breakeven point will realize more than 50¢ of each incremental dollar as profit.

Competition is Severe

Newspapers compete for advertising against many other media in almost all markets. Newspapers in the smallest markets may not have to compete with television, but even there radio is very competitive. Shopper publications, throwaways or other printed advertising exist in most markets. Outdoor billboard and transit advertising are usually available. Direct mail is always competition whether it actually is mailed or distributed door to door. National magazines with local or regional editions have become a new competitive factor in major marketing areas. Local magazines of several types exist in large and some small markets. Premiums, trading stamps, coupons and other promotions take advertising dollars from the media. In large markets television is the big competitor, but for the entire newspaper business it is only the tip of the iceberg (see Tables 8 and 9).

Classifications of Newspaper Advertising

Over the years advertising has been grouped in three classifications by nature of the customer and ad type.

National advertising is that which is sold to national brand manufacturers to promote their products. Newspapers employ representatives to sell advertising space to these national accounts and their advertising agencies. This space usually is sold at a higher rate than other types of advertising.

Local advertising is sold primarily to retail stores and service establishments. More local ads are sold than any other category. Local department stores, general merchandise stores and supermarkets are usually the major buyers of advertising. Newspapers often offer lower ad rates for large users, based on their monthly or annual advertising linage.

Classified advertising is sold to local businesses—many of them in the service field—and directly to individuals. Buyers as well as sellers use classified ads. Businesses frequently advertise for help wanted, and some individuals purchase classified space to advertise for items they are seeking. Classified is run under regular column headings uninterrupted by editorial content. Similar ads are grouped together to make them easy for a reader to find. From this grouping came the term "classified."

Despite its brevity and low cost, classified advertising is highly effective. In a major market, a single classified ad may bring dozens or even hundreds of responses. Individuals use classifieds to sell everything from pets to antiques and from farm equipment to coin collections.

City and state governments place official legal notices in classified sections. Lawyers and investigators use them to trace missing persons; lovers, to exchange greetings.

Most classified advertising has only words without any illustrative material. Other local and national advertising generally has photos or art illustrations and therefore typically is called *display advertising*. Some classified advertising also is sold this way—particularly for real estate and automobiles—and hence is *classified display*.

Newspaper *supplements*, which are preprinted to be distributed with the paper, have existed for many years and contain advertising and editorial material. Depending upon financial arrangements, these supplements often produce a return which the newspaper may classify as advertising revenue.

Preprints

Preprints, or pure advertising supplements distributed by a newspaper, also are a source of revenue. Preprints usually are not produced by a newspaper, but are very much a part of it. The growth in preprints has been spectacular in recent years, and they are now a major source of advertising revenue.

Preprints are generally national or regional in character, although many are placed by local retailers. National chain operations have millions of copies printed commercially and make them available to their local stores. They are frequently printed in full color and on higher grade paper than newsprint, in order to attract readers' attention.

Preprints produce far less revenue for a newspaper than a comparable amount of display advertising linage. However, with preprints there is no composition, printing or paper expense—only the cost of insertion and delivery. Therefore, newspapers develop a preprint rate which more than covers these costs but is generally less than it would cost an advertiser to mail or otherwise deliver the preprint. The newspaper benefits from the revenue received, while advertisers and the consuming public benefit from the efficiency of timely newspaper delivery.

Local Retail Advertising

Newspapers are primarily a local retail advertising medium or, on occasion, a carrier of regional advertising. Retail advertising has always been the largest part of total newspaper advertising revenue. Its importance is indicated in Table 7.

From 1969 through 1975 retail advertising was the fastest growing

Table 7
ADVERTISING REVENUE IN MILLIONS OF DOLLARS

	Retail Advertising	Total Newspaper Advertising	% Retail
1969	3,181	5,714	55.7
1970	3,299	5,704	57.8
1971	3,562	6,198	57.5
1972	3,957	7,008	56.5
1973	4,236	7,595	55.8
1974	4,552	8,001	56.9
1975	4,958	8,442	58.7
1976	5,845	10,205	57.3
1977	6,430 P	11,260 P	57.1 P

P—Projection estimates.
Source: McCann Erickson, Inc.

segment of newspaper advertising, slightly exceeding the growth rate of classified and outpacing that of natural advertising by a considerable margin. However, since 1975 newspapers' national advertising revenues have expanded rapidly. For example, in 1976 national newspaper advertising expenditures expanded almost 23 percent.

Retailers rely on newspapers to move merchandise. No other medium has consistently been so effective. Department and general merchandise stores, food, clothing and other retailers are large users of newspaper advertising. Newspapers cover entire markets for area chain operators, and through zoned pages or sections which are distributed to specific geographic areas, newspapers also can be effective for a one-outlet retailer. Zoned advertising costs less because it goes to only part of a newspaper's circulation. However, the cost per unit of circulation is higher.

Newspapers publish special sections or pages on fashions, food, finance, travel and other subjects which attract both readers and advertisers. Readers generally know where to find various types of advertising in the newspaper and, therefore, it is a ready source of shopping information. Sales promotions and other price-competitive advertising generally are placed primarily in newspapers rather than in other media.

Merrill Lynch, Pierce, Fenner and Smith in its April, 1975 *Overview of the Newspaper Industry* observed, "A look at the relative importance of local and national advertising reveals the general source of the newspaper industry's increasing market share. Local advertising, which accounted for just 38% of total advertising expenditures (all media) in 1963, had risen to almost 45% of the total in 1973. That trend appears to result from two conditions: first, local advertising has been growing at a faster rate than national advertising; and second, some national placement has been shifted to local placement."

As shown in Table 8, newspapers have lost some local advertising to television, but total growth in local advertising has increased newspapers' revenues significantly despite their smaller share of the market.

Table 8

MEDIA SHARES OF LOCAL ADVERTISING DOLLARS
(Millions of Dollars)
1946–1976

	Newspapers	%	Television	%	Radio	%	Other	%	Total	%
1946	917	66.0	-0-	-0-	157	11.3	316	22.7	1,390	100
1955	2,365	62.7	225	6.0	327	8.7	853	22.6	3,770	100
1960	2,903	62.4	280	6.0	428	9.2	1,044	22.4	4,655	100
1965	3,642	61.6	386	6.5	582	9.8	1,300	22.0	5,910	100
1970	4,813	58.7	704	8.6	881	10.7	1,802	22.0	8,200	100
1975	7,221	55.8	1,334	10.5	1,461	11.6	2,865	22.1	12,820	100
1976	8,680	56.7	1,665	10.9	1,636	10.7	3,317	21.7	15,298	100

Source: McCann Erickson, Inc., Newspaper Advertising Bureau—1976 data are preliminary.

The success of print advertising for retailers also has prompted increased competition for newspapers from advertising throw aways or shoppers. Some shopper publications develop into newspapers as they add editorial content and other features. In some markets, newspapers have started their own shoppers, delivering them to all area residences.

High-quality print advertising—much of it in full color—has improved and grown significantly in recent years. Some merchandisers mail quality advertising pieces while others pay to have them delivered by specialized organizations or inserted into newspapers for delivery.

Advertising distributed to only a portion of a newspaper's circulation usually is called zoned advertising, and zoned pages or sections may include localized editorial content. Substantial increases in newsprint cost and advertising rates—coupled with newspaper production flexibility arising from new technology—have accelerated the trend toward both zoned advertising and editorial content.[1]

Table 9

MEDIA SHARES OF NATIONAL ADVERTISING DOLLARS
(Millions of Dollars)
1946–1976

	Newspapers		Television		Radio		Magazines		Other*		Total
		%		%		%		%		%	(100%)
1946	238	12.2	-0-	-0-	298	15.3	405	20.8	1,009	51.7	1,950
1955	712	13.2	810	15.1	218	4.1	763	14.2	2,877	53.5	5,380
1960	778	10.7	1,347	18.4	265	3.6	975	13.3	3,940	53.9	7,305
1965	784	8.4	2,129	22.8	335	3.6	1,232	13.2	4,860	52.0	9,340
1970	891	7.9	2,892	25.5	427	3.8	1,354	11.9	5,786	51.0	11,350
1975	1,220	7.9	3,929	25.8	519	3.4	1,465	9.6	8,205	53.3	15,410
1976	1,525	8.3	4,910	26.8	592	3.2	1,775	9.7	9,530	52.1	18,305

Source: McCann Erickson, Inc., Newspaper Advertising Bureau—1976 data are preliminary.
*"Other' includes farm publications, direct mail, business papers, outdoor and miscellaneous advertising categories.

National Advertising

National advertising always has been the smallest portion of newspaper ad linage. However, because national advertising generally has been sold at a higher rate than local advertising, it has been an important part of the picture. Fluctuations in national advertising linage have more than a proportionate impact on newspaper earnings. Table 9 provides some insight into changes in market shares since World War II.

In the past two decades, television apparently has reduced newspapers' share of national advertising by about 40 percent. However, television's impact on radio and magazines was more serious than its effect on newspapers. It appears that television's penetration into national advertising income has leveled off at around 26 percent.

During recent years newspapers have attracted what is called *cooperative advertising*—promotional dollars made available by manufacturers to local distributors and retailers. In a cooperative program, the advertising space is sold by the newspaper to a local retailer who is then reimbursed by the national manufacturer for at least part of the ad's cost. Newspapers are increasing efforts to serve this part of the advertising market.

Television advertising has been dominated largely by national accounts in the food, drug, beverage, auto and cosmetic industries. Cigarette advertising was very important for television until banned, and newspapers have regained substantial amounts of it. Liquor advertising also is prohibited on television and, therefore, has been significant for newspapers. Very few newspapers ban liquor ads.

One challenge to the newspaper business is to develop more effective ad sales techniques. Other media, particularly television, radio and magazines, have demographic analyses of their audiences and "cost per 1000" (CPM) data. They have convinced many national accounts and agencies to use such data when selecting advertising media. Many newspapers still are developing equally sophisticated sales information. Newspapers traditionally have cited "net paid circulation" rather than *total* number of readers and, consequently, have somewhat underestimated their audiences in "cost per 1000" comparisons. Most newspapers are upgrading their selling efforts with appropriate research data and are improving their competitive position among the media.

The wide variety of advertising formats and specifications used by various newspapers had, until recently, been a problem for newspapers in attracting national advertising. In 1975, the American Newspaper Publishers Association (ANPA) Newspaper Format Committee adopted a plan which set up six standardized size groupings for the advertising makeup dimensions of newspapers. In preparing this plan, the committee discovered that U.S. newspapers had been using at least 214 different formats of which 103 were "one of a kind." This proliferation of formats had discouraged some advertisers from using newspapers.

Classified Advertising

Classified advertising pages are uniquely interesting to many readers and advertisers because they contain death and birth notices, lost and found, personal ads and other information. Many newspaper readers are habitual scanners of these pages. Because they are organized efficiently, they are effective sales agents for businesses and the public at large. In effect, classified pages contain the essence of the "Yellow Pages" updated and revised every day.

Despite its relatively low cost, classified advertising generally produces of higher profit per page than retail advertising and these pages can increase without requiring a corresponding increase in editorial content. Many newspapers exclude classified pages when computing their advertising/editorial content ratio.

Classified advertising usually is sold both by telephone solicitors and street-sales personnel, while most retail advertising is sold by salesmen who call on their accounts daily or weekly. Although sales cost per page of classified ads is generally higher than for other advertising, revenue per page is also greater. Rates are structured to encourage repetition of an ad for several days, weeks or months, with other incentives for annual volume. Classified revenue per page also is increased by running more columns per page than for display advertising. Thus many newspapers have 9 or 10 classified advertising columns per page compared with 8 or 6 columns on a display page. Inventive classified sales managers continue to develop new uses for classified advertising. The "garage sale," for example, has become a major new classification. Because classified columns can be easily adapted to new living styles, merchandising trends and reader-to-reader communications, they probably will be increasingly important to newspapers' advertising income.

Conclusion

The growth of television eroded newspapers' share of all advertising. In addition, television is a major competitor for a newspaper reader's time. This competition accounts for some of the decline in the number who read two or more newspapers each day.

However, television is now a relatively mature industry, and newspapers are increasingly sophisticated competitors. For example, since 1963 newspapers have captured a stable proportion of all advertising expenditures. Their share of the advertising dollar, in fact, is slightly higher today than it was 15 years ago.

Newspapers have faced challenges in maintaining circulation. Cost increases have led to increased circulation rates which usually, or at least temporarily, cause circulation to decline. Vigorous marketing efforts, a slowing of cost increases and improved efficiency should help to stabilize circulation prices in the future, enhancing the growth of newspaper circulation.

NOTES
Chapter 7

[1] For a more detailed discussion of zoned advertising and news, see Chapter 10, pp. 148–149.

8

Newspaper Costs and Control

RAPID INFLATION has made cost control a top priority of American industry. This is especially true in the newspaper business because of exceptionally large cost increases for newsprint and personnel.

Newspapers have a unique cost situation. They are sold to consumers at less than production cost. The sale of advertising generates the majority of revenue essential to profitable operation.

When newspapers appear to be packed with advertising one or two days a week, some observers presume handsome profits. But advertising must be timed to shopping habits, not to the most efficient newspaper production schedule. When a daily newspaper publishes five to seven days a week—depending on its size and market—there are slack advertising days and sometimes weeks when operating expenses exceed total revenue. This, combined with the uncertainty of future revenues and costs, makes cost control an essential element of newspaper management.

Goals of Cost Control

Minimizing costs must not jeopardize the product quality which is essential to building paid circulation and to fulfilling a newspaper's social responsibilities.

Because of increasing newsprint prices, wage rates and other costs, newspaper prices have mounted steadily. As of the beginning of 1977, 1488 or 85.3 percent of all U. S. daily newspapers sold for 15 cents a copy or less. However, the vast majority of those papers sold for 15 cents. Unless a newspaper is of superior quality at 15 cents a day, it cannot compete in an economy-conscious market when the public can obtain, without *direct* charge,[1] an assortment of entertainment and information from broadcast media and a growing proliferation of free shopper newspapers.

Within this competitive environment, newspaper management seeks to produce a quality product at a reasonable cost. The keys to success are excellence and efficiency.

The Nature of Newspaper Costs

Newspaper costs can be viewed in a variety of ways. Many newspapers figure costs by function such as news-editorial; advertising; composition; some combination of engraving, camera, stereotyping and platemaking (depending upon the type of printing process used); pressroom; circulation and distribution, and administration and overhead. Each functional area or "cost center" has target goals and budgeted costs for achieving them.

Costs frequently are classified as variable or fixed. *Variable costs* are those which tend to vary directly with volume—size and circulation of the newspaper. Included among them are newsprint, purchased supplements and production supplies—as shown in Table 1. Because these costs, by definition, vary directly with the size of a newspaper, they may constitute as little as 15 percent of all costs for a small daily or 35 percent or more of the total cost of a large metropolitan.

Direct fixed costs are incurred regardless of daily volume. They are "direct" in that they are incurred in the daily creation, printing and delivery of a newspaper. They are "fixed" in that they do not vary considerably with volume. Labor is the largest direct fixed cost. Salaries and wages, together with employe benefits, may constitute over 50 percent of all costs, especially for a small newspaper. Other direct fixed costs include contractual expenses for news and picture-wire services, features, press association assessments, press and mechanical maintenance and utility charges.

Indirect fixed costs do not vary with volume and are only indirectly related to daily operations. For example, depreciation of plant and equipment, interest on debt and certain administrative salaries are incurred whether a paper is produced or not. These costs are frequently difficult to allocate to specific cost centers such as news-editorial, circu-

Table 1

OPERATING COSTS FOR A DAILY AND SUNDAY NEWSPAPER OF 12–18,000 CIRCULATION

	Total	Daily	Sunday
Variable Costs:			
Newsprint—Sunday supplements	$ 106,762	$ —	$106,762
Newsprint—Other	740,033	646,334	93,699
Ink—color	3,241	2,880	361
Ink—black & white	12,318	8,122	4,196
Outside printing	154,622	—	154,622
Purchased sections	85,093	40,640	44,453
Wire and Wrappers	6,973	4,112	2,861
Total variable costs	1,109,042	702,088	406,954
Variable costs as a percent of all operating costs	29.8%	29.0%	31.4%
Direct-fixed costs:			
Editorial	317,830	246,107	71,723
Engraving	15,484	11,614	3,870
Composing	330,189	221,993	108,196
Sterotyping	44,472	33,753	10,719
Press & mechanical maintenance	301,102	206,133	94,969
Mailroom, drivers, auto	292,739	171,819	120,920
Circulation: sales	91,542	52,180	39,362
Circulation: distribution	424,636	235,502	189,134
Advertising: retail	53,512	37,621	15,891
Advertising: general	67,696	48,622	19,074
Advertising: classified	49,417	30,986	18,431
Dispatch & make-up	18,655	13,157	5,498
Bookkeeping—circulation	2,119	1,201	918
Bookkeeping—display	6,543	4,864	1,679
Bookkeeping—classified	18,806	11,662	7,144
Bookkeeping—credit	20,939	14,175	6,764
Total direct-fixed costs	2,055,681	1,341,389	714,292
Direct-fixed costs as a percent of all operating costs	55.3%	55.4%	55.1%
Indirect-fixed costs:			
General & administrative	478,165	338,815	139,350
Depreciation	76,573	40,379	36,194
Total indirect-fixed costs	554,738	379,194	175,544
Indirect-fixed costs as a percent of all operating costs	14.9%	15.6%	13.5%

Source: Adopted from *Newspaper Controller,* May 1975.

lation or production. This is especially true of interest charges and executive salaries.

With rapid modernization of newspaper processes and equipment, depreciation expenses are becoming an increasingly significant proportion of all costs. If borrowed capital is used to finance new plant and equipment, interest expenses also may be large.

Controllable Costs

While many costs are classified as either direct or indirect fixed, they can be influenced by management decisions. In this sense, they are at least partially controllable. Although labor costs are relatively fixed, decisions relating to labor-saving technology, overtime policies and changes in staffing can have a substantial impact on future labor charges. If new technology is purchased, future depreciation charges also will be affected.

In recent years the greatest cost control efforts have centered on new technology and newsprint. A newspaper cannot control the price of a ton of newsprint, but it can exercise some control over how much newsprint it uses. The rising price of newsprint has become a catalyst for closer control of all newspaper costs. A need to limit price increases and to maintain profitability has caused some newspapers to reduce their supplemental wire services, syndicated columns, employe picnics, unprofitable circulation and other activities.

Problems in Controlling Costs

A major newspaper cost problem is that a newspaper must be equipped and staffed to handle volume levels that vary greatly from day to day. Unlike most manufacturing enterprises, it cannot inventory the product and lay off employes when advertising space or circulation temporarily decline. Production staffs, which are only a small proportion of all employes, can be geared to daily volume to a limited degree; but the news-editorial, advertising, circulation and business departments cannot. For a variety of reasons, no editor can say to a reporter, "There isn't going to be much news this week, therefore you're temporarily laid off."

A second cost problem is the difficulty of measuring the value of a specific feature or activity. Is the expenditure for a given supplement or syndicated column economically justified? Does sponsorship of a boat show ultimately pay for itself in public goodwill and advertising sales? Will a recommended circulation promotion be sufficiently productive? How profitable is an investment in new photocomposition equipment likely to be?

Other problems faced by some newspapers are agreements made during union negotiations which limit management's ability to use efficiently new labor-saving technology. Such agreements have included arrangements to reduce production personnel only by attrition—retirement, death, disability or voluntary resignation. Some newspapers have negotiated lump-sum payments for early retirement in order to reduce personnel levels.

Cost Control Strategies

Recognizing that a newspaper must be profitable to remain in operation and that it must improve quality, attract capital and meet its obligations to the community, management has sought to improve cost control. While there is no one strategy to do this, several concepts and techniques have proved useful:

Involvement. In establishing budgets and cost controls, everyone in a decision-making position involving costs should be consulted and should have a thorough understanding of reasons for cost controls.

Validity. Cost controls must be reasonable; efforts to reach market and performance objectives must be realistically funded.

Communication. All employes should be encouraged to be cost-and-efficiency-conscious, but not "penny-wise and pound-foolish."

Waste-avoidance. Resources are becoming increasingly scarce and expensive; for both ecological and economic reasons, the waste of energy, paper and other resources must be reduced as much as possible.

Measurability. Accurate and timely measures of costs are necessary for effective control.

Cost-benefit ratios. To the greatest extent possible, each expenditure should be justified by its value to a newspaper or its community.

Flexibility. Budgets and cost controls cannot be so rigid that flexibility needed to adjust to extenuating circumstances is lost.

Accountability. Each executive and department should be accountable for those costs incurred under his or her direction.

Advance planning. Effective cost control is anticipatory, that is, both goals and costs should be carefully planned well in advance whenever possible.

Contingency planning. Plans should be made for unexpected events such as a rise in newsprint cost or an unanticipated advertising decline.

In considering implementation of these cost-control concepts and tactics, it is useful to examine some of the current practices of U.S. newspapers.

Editorial Costs

In general, American industry has been weak in communicating to employes the importance of cost controls. Newspapers are no exception. Until recently news departments rarely were consulted in establishing budgets and cost controls, even though editorial decisions significantly influence such variable and direct fixed costs as manpower, purchased services and newsprint use—the latter is controlled by establishment of "news hole" standards.

Generally, the "news hole"—the space allocated to news—is based on a formula developed by experience. Most newspapers have a guaranteed minimum news hole which varies from day to day according to advertising volume. The number of columns guaranteed the news department may vary from paper to paper because of competitive factors. The purpose of a minimum is to insure that each edition will carry sufficient news and feature material to achieve editorial quality. A minimum standard helps news department planning by guaranteeing that space will be available. Newspapers also set maximum limits, but an extraordinary news development sometimes requires a news hole even larger than "maximum." On the other hand, the "minimum" news-hole space may not be used when news flow is light or such features as stock market tables are unavailable because of holidays. An example of news hole and advertising allocation is provided in Table 2.

Although costly, a newspaper may invest in an unusually large news hole to attract additional subscribers and advertisers. If successful, this investment can allow the newspaper to maintain the absolute size of the news hole while reducing its proportion of the newspaper to a profitable level. For example, a new daily is not likely to attract much advertising especially if another newspaper already serves its market. By having a relatively large news hole, it may be able to develop circulation necessary to attract a sizable advertising volume. In other words, a newspaper often invests in editorial quality, not just to achieve excellence, but also to improve its market penetration and competitive position.

A newspaper's news-editorial costs generally range from about 9 percent of total revenue for a 260,000 circulation to 13–15 percent for newspapers under 25,000 circulation. As a percentage of total costs, news-editorial budgets range from around 14 percent for larger papers to 17–22 percent for smaller newspapers. The inverse relationship between percentage of cost and circulation results primarily from economies of scale. It takes no longer for a reporter to prepare a story for a 260,000-circulation paper than for one of 25,000 circulation. This does not mean that large newspapers are more profitable; they have other costs which rise with size, such as newsprint. And, a big-city reporter usually earns more than his or her smaller-town colleagues.

Table 2

DAILY STANDARDS FOR SPACE ALLOCATION

Morning Daily Minimums: Monday, 100; Tuesday, 120; Wednesday, 127 Thursday, 143; Friday, 125; Saturday, 110

Adv. Columns		Pages per Issue	News Columns	
Min.	Max.		Min.	Max.
53	64	16	64	75
65	76	18	68	79
77	88	20	72	83
89	100	22	76	87
101	112	24	80	91
113	124	26	84	95
125	136	28	88	99
137	148	30	92	103
149	160	32	96	107
161	172	34	100	111
173	184	36	104	115
185	196	38	108	119
197	208	40	112	123
209	220	42	116	127
221	232	44	120	131
233	244	46	124	135
245	256	48	128	139
257	270	50	130	143
271	286	52	130	145
287	302	54	130	145
303	318	56	130	145
319	334	58	130	145
335	350	60	130	145
351	366	62	130	145
367	382	64	130	145
383	398	66	130	145
399	414	68	130	145
415	430	70	130	145
431	446	72	130	145
447	462	74	130	145
463	478	76	130	145

Source: The *Richmond* (Va.) *Times Dispatch,* a newspaper with a daily circulation of 132,000.

In controlling costs, editors must determine the type of news-editorial product that will best serve readers' needs. That determination will suggest the size and nature of the staff needed to produce the product. Management also defines, by periodic review, the distribution territory most efficient from a cost standpoint and most beneficial to advertisers. This territory generally is known as the "prime market area" because it is this segment of the total market that is most attractive to a newspaper's major advertisers. Except for newspapers seeking regional prestige, distribution limits can help control costs. Revenue from subscribers outside the "prime market area" often falls short of the additional costs of serving such fringe circulation.

Newsprint Costs

Newsprint prices have doubled in the past ten years and have almost tripled since 1950. Figure 1 shows newsprint prices per ton since 1925. As previously mentioned, the recent escalation of prices has prompted conservation efforts. In addition to curtailing fringe circulation, newspapers have conserved paper by altering page width; converting from an eight- to a six-column format, using smaller news holes; standardizing advertising formats, curtailing free distribution; controlling press overruns, and eliminating waste. The largest U.S. user of newsprint, the *Los Angeles Times,* reduced its page width three-quarters of an inch, went to a six-column format and slashed its newsprint bill about $4.2 million a year.[2] It is estimated that U.S. daily newspaper's conservation practices saved 459,000 tons of newsprint in 1975.[3] At an average $270 per ton, newsprint conservation saved about $124 million during that year. With higher prices today, the savings are now even greater.

The controlling of newsprint costs imposes special problems for editors and advertising managers who must skillfully tailor a quality product for their community despite reduced available space. The editor often must decide whether an edition will have two more pages to provide space for an important story or a late ad, or whether an ad cancellation permits a two-page reduction. When newsprint was $100 a ton that decision was not nearly as significant as when the price exceeds $300 a ton.

Newsprint is the largest variable cost because of fluctuations in advertising volume and circulation. However, among all newspaper costs, it ranks second to labor in magnitude.

Personnel Costs and Productivity

Personnel costs often represent 50 percent or more of a newspaper's total expenses. These costs have risen steadily because of inflation that

Figure 1

The Trend of Newsprint Prices Per Ton 1925-1976

(Annual Averages Delivered at New York City)

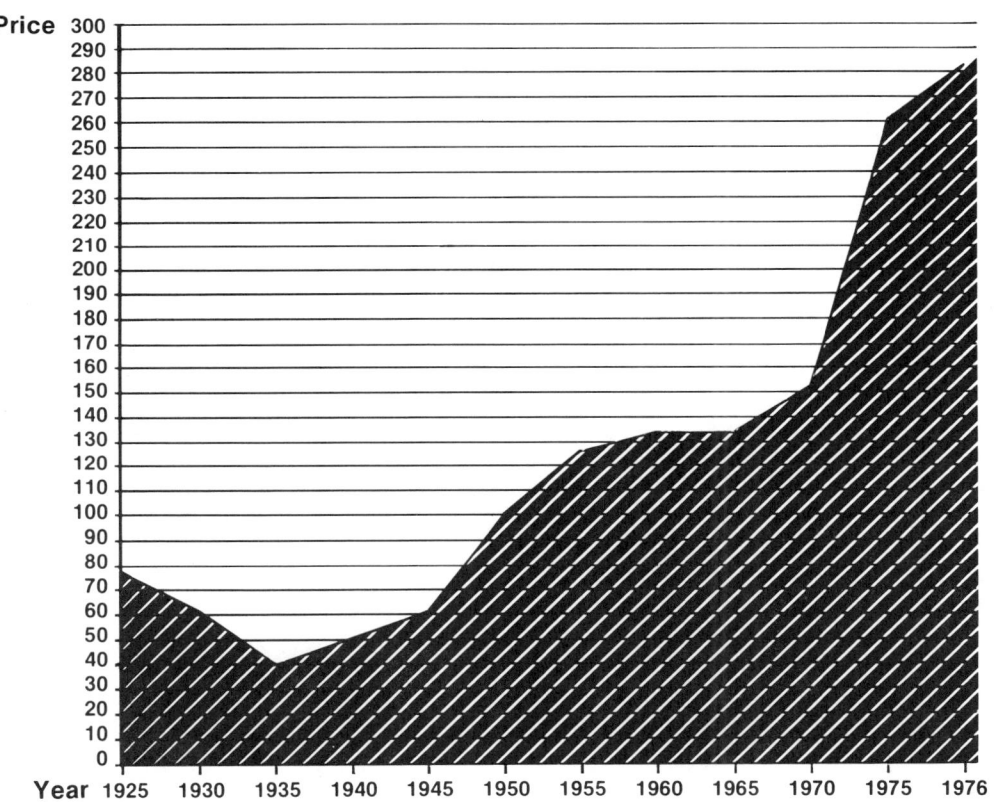

Source: Newsprint Information Committee

sent consumer prices soaring over 80 percent from 1965 through 1976.

Until the late 1960s, newspapers generally were slower than other manufacturing businesses in attempting to cut labor costs. For most of this century, in fact, newspapers were produced—and a few still are—with improved versions of linotype, stereotype and press equipment invented in the nineteenth century.[4]

The adoption of new newspaper technology during the 1960s and 1970s has greatly increased productivity. Many newspapers trimmed composition department manpower, reducing composing costs 25 to 35 percent. Newspapers without union contracts were able, through attrition and early retirements, to reduce manpower (a direct-fixed cost) fairly quickly. However most big-city newspapers had to renegotiate union contracts in order to take advantage of manpower savings made possible by new technology. Newspaper management now is receptive to technological advances in all departments.

The measuring of productivity is far from an exact science, but a consistent program to evaluate manpower needs and employe utilization helps control cost and maintain employe morale. Research has shown that low employe morale often stems from poor supervision and work schedules that do not keep people busy.

One study covering business in general showed that an average worker has nothing to do at least 17 percent of a work day and wastes another 28 percent because of poor management. James A. Skidmore, Jr., president of Science Management Corporation, a New Jersey consulting firm, reported, "employes know that they are not contributing the way they could under proper direction." Figure 2 shows the financial consequence of just one hour of wasted time a day.[5]

As Peter Drucker, an authority on management has stated, "fixed human assets" must be managed.[6] The ablest salesman, reporter or any other employe has only two major resources—time and talent. There is a direct relationship between the amount of time an employe has for work and what is accomplished. Paid employe time not available for productive work is a major, though usually hidden, cost. This means that management needs to know how much work time actually is not used productively and why—for example, a salesman may spend two-thirds of his or her time on paperwork rather than on selling.

Frequently, productivity can be increased simply by reallocating workloads. Circulation departments can become more productive by assigning creative sales people to the task of increasing circulation and relieving them of the routine servicing of day-to-day problems. Editors can use newer reporters to gather routine information, giving experienced reporters more time to develop stories that will improve a newspaper's quality and usefulness. Top management can increase its productivity by wisely delegating duties and not spending extraordinary amounts of time on small problems.

A second, and perhaps more important, key to productivity is motivation. A newspaper can cut costs by motivating employes to be both productive and cost-conscious. Among the many factors involved are self-esteem in one's work, management's known recognition of the importance of each employe, regard for superior performance and general recognition of the importance of efficiency.

As emphasized by William O. Taylor, president of *The Boston Globe*,

Figure 2

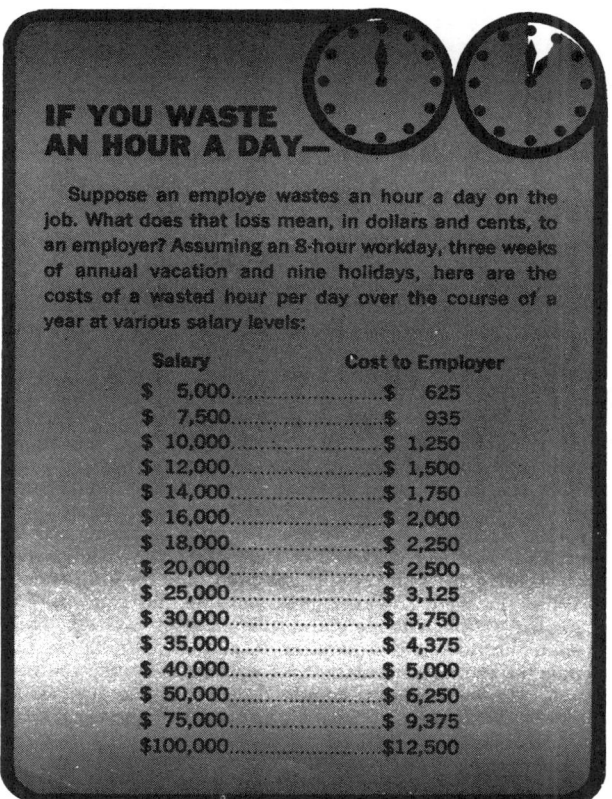

"Reprinted from 'U. S. News & World Report.' Copyright 1973 U. S. News & World Report, Inc."

effective supervision of personnel is management's biggest challenge in bringing about successful cost control.[7]

Measurability

Roy W. Anderson, general manager of *The News American* in Baltimore, has pointed out, "A key to achieving efficiency in control of costs, and attaining objectives of the newspaper is best summed up in one word . . . 'measurability.' "[8] To Robert G. Marbut, president of Harte-Hanks, Communications, Inc., the most sensible way to control costs and to improve operational efficiency without weakening the product is to take a preventive approach. In addition to fiscal planning, Marbut points out, "There must be a reporting system to tell the publisher where he is in order for him to know how far off base he is at any point in time. The next step is the most painful—the self-discipline to get back on the track as soon as one discovers he is off track."[9]

The Gannett Company, owner of some 70 dailies representing a good cross-section of American newspapers, has an elaborate financial reporting system that compares actual results to forecasts in each accounting period. This system is designed, "(1) to provide a means of generating a timely set of profit-planning reports, and (2) provide on demand a means of testing, for management analysis, the impact of proposed and possible changes in the forecasts regardless of the source of these changes."[10]

Communications and Coordination

Statistical information is worth little unless it is analyzed consistently and unless results are communicated to department heads and key employes able to act on the information. Key people also should communicate with *all employes,* many of whom can spot wasteful procedures ignored by supervisors or not apparent to management. A good cost-saver's cash award system more than pays for itself through cost-cutting suggestions, and provides an extra dividend in better morale through employe participation.

Coordination of planning among department heads is essential. If news and advertising departments have special projects that will affect work loads in the production department, scheduling of press units and distribution operations, the projects should be reviewed by all managers concerned as far ahead of time as possible. Timely coordination often permits work assignments to be scheduled without costly overtime or hiring temporary employes.

Contingency Planning

Sound cost control can be upset by unforeseen developments. Therefore, cost control strategy should include contingency plans for quick response to changing conditions. When possible, expenses should be brought in line with budget allocations. If there is an unexpected drop in revenue, budgets should be revised downward, if possible.

All department heads and those key sub-department chiefs who are responsible for putting contingency plans into operation should be involved in formulating them. Once contingency plans are made, they should be reviewed periodically and updated as conditions require, even though they have not had to be implemented.

In 1972, newspapers were faced with a substantial postal rate increase. The situation was particularly severe for the *Louisville Courier-Journal* which distributed 40 percent of its daily circulation by mail. As rates went up for editions sent outside the Louisville metropolitan area, advertising content was more than halved, cutting both postage and newsprint costs. The paper kept its costs in line and still maintained its policy of being a regional paper serving Kentucky and Indiana.[11] Without such contingency action, the *Courier-Journal* would have found it highly difficult to serve distant mail subscribers.

Contingency cost-cutting plans, from reducing personnel by attrition or layoffs to trimming telephone bills and travel expenses, must be accomplished without significantly jeopardizing product quality. One of the ways to maintain quality is to eliminate expenses that do not produce a meaningful result. One such strategy is to pull out of circulation areas of marginal benefit to advertisers, but only if it can be accomplished without lowering ad rates. Another move is to call a temporary halt to non-revenue-producing promotion projects and to defer capital improvements.

In implementing cost reduction plans, all costs considered routine should be thoroughly reviewed. Big expenses are monitored constantly, but "hidden" and often needless costs perpetuated by habit represent sizable sums on a cumulative basis—travel expense, convention trips, excessive complimentary or office distribution of free papers, for example. Pruning techniques, rather than hack and slash tactics, should be used to eliminate such costs.

Conclusion

Cost-control strategy involves: Efficient use of *every* employe's work time; measurement of management and employe performance with rewards for increasing productivity and for efficiently executing cost controls; effective control of newsprint usage; and early warning when costs are out of control. Besides maintaining adequate records, all departmental managers must be alert to sudden changes from normal operating conditions.

Controlling costs also requires contingency planning and the self-discipline to quickly implement correctional programs when expenses get out of hand or revenues decline. The ultimate goal of cost control is to eliminate waste and unnecessary expenses. In so doing, a newspaper must maintain its financial independence without jeopardizing the fundamental objective of furnishing readers with a quality news and advertising product.

NOTES
Chapter 8

[1] Television and radio are not free. There is the cost of equipment, maintenance and electricity plus, in the case of cable television, direct monthly fees for the service.

[2] A $4.2 million saving at newsprint prices prevailing as of October, 1974.

[3] Jon G. Udell, *Dynamics of U. S. Daily Newspapers and Newsprint Consumption,* American Newspaper Publishers Association (Reston, Va.), Newsprint & Traffic Bulletin, No. 2, January 21, 1976, p. 17.

[4] Information and development and adoption of new technology is presented in Chapters 6 and 10.

[5] "How to Make the Most of Your Time," U.S. News and World Report, December 3, 1973.

[6] "Managing Capital Productivity," Peter F. Drucker, *The Wall Street Journal,* July 24, 1975.

[7] Letter from William O. Taylor to contributing author.

[8] Letter from Roy W. Anderson to contributing author.

[9] Letter from Robert G. Marbut to contributing author.

[10] *Editor & Publisher* (March 10, 1975), p. 40.

[11] Information from George Gill, general manager, in interview with contributing author.

9

Employe Relations in the Newspaper Business

Employe relations can be defined simply as the art of working effectively with people. A broader definition might encompass all methods by which a business or other employer recruits, hires, trains and maintains employes who will put forth their best efforts to contribute to the success of the enterprise.

The subject goes by a number of different names. It has been called variously industrial relations, personnel relations, labor relations, employment relations, employer-employe relations, labor-management relations, human relations, personnel management and personnel administration. Textbook writers differ in the application of these titles. For the purposes of this chapter, *employe relations* will include labor and personnel relations.

The term *labor relations* is generally used in connection with negotiation and administration of collective bargaining agreements which regulate wages, fringe benefits and working conditions for employe groups who have designated a union as their representative. *Personnel relations* generally refers to all aspects of employe relations which are not governed by collective bargaining agreements or employment contracts.

Unionization

The extent of unionization among newspaper employes varies widely from city to city and even among individual newspapers in the same city. Some large metropolitan newspapers, like *The New York Times*, may have as many as 14 or 15 different unions representing various employe groups. Others, like *The Los Angeles Times* and *The Miami Herald*, have no unions. The largest newspaper union is the International Typographical Union, which historically has represented composing room employes. In recent years it has embraced some editorial people and others. Other crafts often represented by unions are photoengravers, stereotypers, pressmen, mailers, paper handlers, electricians, machinists and building service employes. The Newspaper Guild originally started as a union of professional journalists—reporters and copy editors. However, it has expanded to include clerical, sales, circulation and maintenance employes in some areas. The Guild has contracts with about 135 dailies. The Typographical Union has contracts with about 450.

Newspapers are particularly vulnerable to any strikes which *prevent* daily publication. Unlike a nuts and bolts factory, a newspaper cannot stockpile news or advertising. An edition lost is permenently forfeit. The lost advertising and circulation revenue cannot be regained. The public loses, too; people do not get their newspapers.

Newspaper persons feel strongly that they have a moral obligation to keep publishing regularly and on schedule. One of the most effective ways to assure regular publication without work interruption is to maintain good employe relations.

Importance of Employe Relations

The process of creating good employe relations includes maintaining a productive, informed and loyal employe group by selecting and training capable people and providing good working conditions, competent leadership, adequate compensation, recognition of superior performance, opportunity for growth and development and a reasonable degree of financial security for an employe and his or her family.

Implementing that kind of employe-relations program under collective bargaining is not necessarily easy, even though a company may have a basic personnel relations philosophy of concern for each employe as an individual. When day-to-day working conditions are governed by a contract, sometimes negotiated by outside third parties, it can be extremely difficult, and sometimes even illegal, to recognize individual employe needs, skills and differences.

One should reject the myth that newspaper personnel are somehow different from other employes. Perhaps we can blame Ben Hecht and the movies for an erroneous stereotype of the typical newspaper employe. His "Front Page" gave us a cigar-chewing, hard-boiled city editor, a playboy reporter solving murder mysteries in his spare time, a roaring press churning screaming headlines and a few freckle-faced kids yelling "Extra!" on the streets. That just isn't the way it happens in real life. People who work for newspapers have the same basic needs and desires as those who work for banks or breweries. Nevertheless, for its size, the newspaper business does involve a great variety of skilled specialists. It takes hard work, good timing and whole-hearted cooperation from a great many specialists in a number of different departments to write, produce and deliver at each edition time the equivalent of a completely new book.

Although the percentages may vary somewhat with organization size, an average daily newspaper has about 15 percent of its employes producing and editing news and features, 10 percent selling and processing advertising, another 15 percent in business office or administrative positions, 12 percent in circulation sales and delivery, and about 48 percent in the various production and maintenance departments.

Maintaining a favorable employe relations climate with such a diverse group of specialists is a formidable task. But it is necessary—not only because of the obligation to publish regularly without interruption, but also because of the magnitude of labor costs and the need for productivity improvement.

Newspapers Are Labor Intensive

The newspaper business is "labor intensive." In the automobile industry about 14 cents out of every sales dollar is spent for payroll. In steel it is about 22 cents. In textiles it is less than 20 cents, and in petroleum it is only 6 cents. Although there is some variation among newspapers of various sizes, a typical metropolitan newspaper spends about 37 cents out of every revenue dollar for payroll alone. Another 5 cents goes for employe benefits not included in payroll. The magnitude of a newspaper's payroll and employe benefit costs underscores the extreme importance of employe relations in the newspaper business.

Good employe relations become even more important in an atmosphere of technological change.[1] Most people instinctively resist change. They particularly resist changes they do not completely understand, and they rebel against changes they think may jeopardize their own job security.

Figure 1

Distribution, Newspaper Work Force

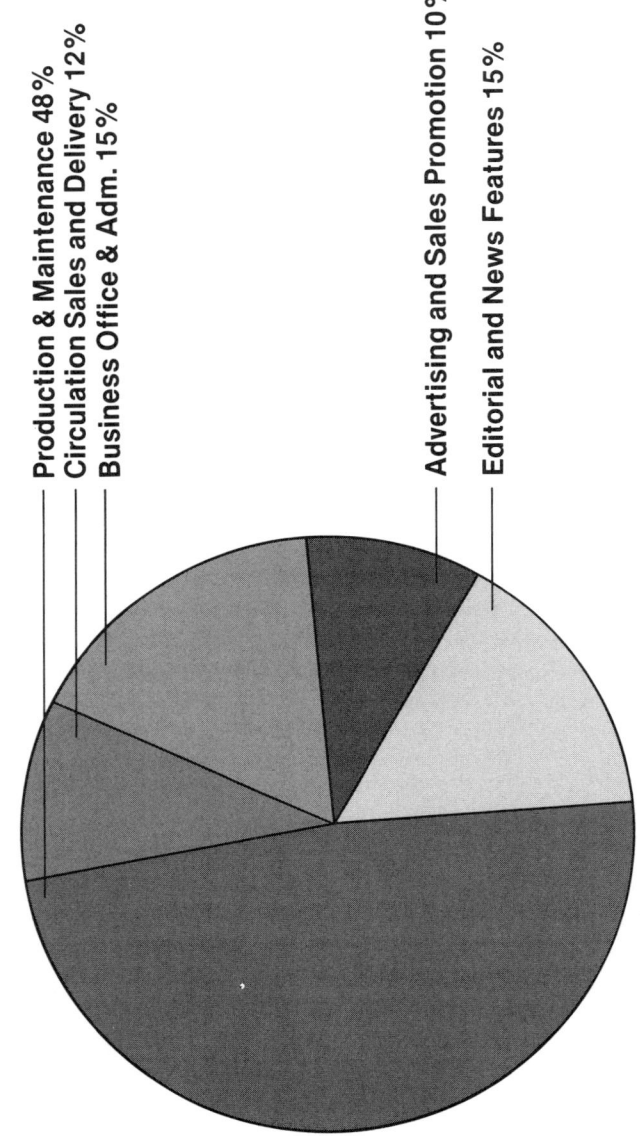

Source: Newspapers, Inc. Accounting Records & ANPA

Figure 2

Distribution of a Revenue Dollar

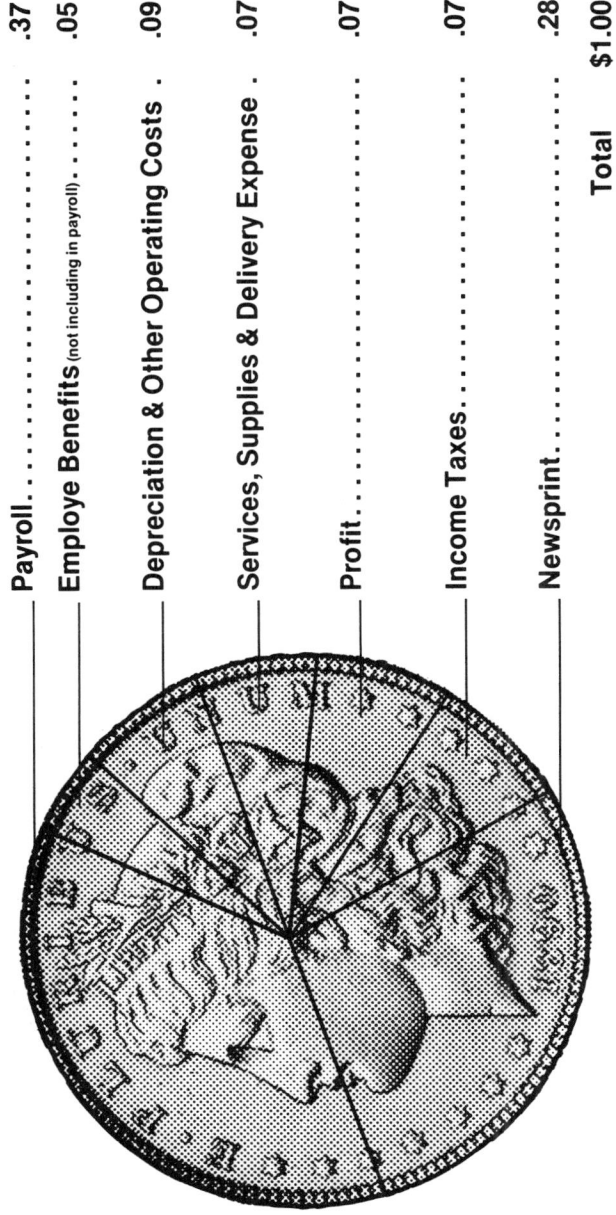

Payroll	.37
Employe Benefits (not including in payroll)	.05
Depreciation & Other Operating Costs	.09
Services, Supplies & Delivery Expense	.07
Profit	.07
Income Taxes	.07
Newsprint	.28
Total	$1.00

Source: U.S. Department of Commerce, ANPA and Newspapers, Inc.

For many years productivity lagged in the newspaper business. There are many definitions of the word "productivity." It can be defined as "output per man hour of work." From a financial standpoint, it also can be defined as "cost per unit produced." In the newspaper business productivity may be viewed as "cost per page produced" or "man hours per page produced."

Considering its nature, the newspaper enterprise is surprisingly efficient. Because of daily variations in size and content, the development of a newspaper does not lend itself to a standardized assembly-line operation. It is a giant jig-saw puzzle—and a new one with every edition.

Is Compensation Adequate?

The question frequently arises whether newspapers pay sufficient wages and salaries to attract competent people. Statistics vary somewhat with newspaper size, but compensation per man hour increased 62 percent in all U.S. manufacturing between 1967 and 1974. Compensation per man hour rose 72 percent in the average metropolitan newspaper during the same period. Few newspapers suffer from a lack of job applicants, and the number of journalism students has risen rapidly in recent years. Although it may not have been true some years ago, it appears that today's newspaper wages and salaries generally are adequate to attract and hold good people.

But, compensation is only one part of employe relations, and not always the most important part. A high pay scale, a short work week, the best employe benefit program in the world and wall-to-wall carpeting will not, in themselves, motivate employes to sustain a high level of effort. In addition, employes need to feel that they have:
- Meaningful work in a worthwhile enterprise;
- Respect and understanding from superiors;
- Honest communications from management;
- Opportunity for security, learning, and advancement.

It has been said that the proper mixture to make any newspaper run smoothly and successfully consists of two-thirds people and one-third machinery. It does not make sense to invest many thousands of dollars in new machinery and practically nothing in employe relations. If one buys 25 new typewriters of the same make and model, they will be practically identical and interchangeable. When one hires 25 people, no two are alike. If they are interchanged, they will produce different results. Each one has different abilities, ambitions, skills, interests and attitudes. Each one presents an invitation and opportunity to fully utilize individual abilities, to satisfy personal ambitions, to sharpen specialized skills, to capitalize on particular interests—and hopefully to develop a reasonable degree of loyalty to a newspaper employer.

A good overall employe relations program has to be dynamic—it must anticipate change, stimulate progress, accelerate improvement and encourage increased productivity.

In some circles, the word "productivity" has taken on an odious connotation. Gains in productivity are not achieved as a result of people working harder. They are not achieved by a "speed-up." Productivity increases in newspapers and other businesses result from the application of efficient work systems and processes, employe morale, and from the utilization of new equipment and methods which avoid wasted effort.

Effective Collective Bargaining

Effective collective bargaining is an essential part of employe relations in a unionized newspaper. People join unions for several reasons. One is that they crave recognition as human beings and want to be treated with respect. They seek acceptance by fellow workers and a feeling of security from union representation. Yet a union depends for its existence on the company. If there is no company, there is no union. Union dues come out of wages provided by the company. Union members have security only to the extent that a company is able to provide jobs.

A newspaper's responsibilities to unionized employes cannot begin and end at the bargaining table.

Planning for labor negotiations should be a year-round job. Actual sessions at the bargaining table can be helped or hindered by the overall labor relations climate which has been established either by proper planning or by the lack of it. Preparation for collective bargaining involves gathering all relevant data, and then planning to present it much as a lawyer prepares for a trial. Collective-bargaining sessions in themselves have become a kind of ritual in which both sides exchange arguments in a protracted series of meetings. One of the negotiators' most important task is to convince union members that their representatives have obtained the best possible settlement from the company. The real settlement is not reached at the bargaining table, but at a union meeting when members vote on the company proposal. Under such circumstances, the success or failure of all the collective bargaining sessions must stand or fall on the good faith and sales ability of four or five union representatives who present the negotiated contract proposal at a union meeting. To many newspaper executives, the system seems tenuous and insecure.

Figure 3
**Employe Benefits
Average Annual Cost Per Employe
In Typical Metropolitan Newspaper**

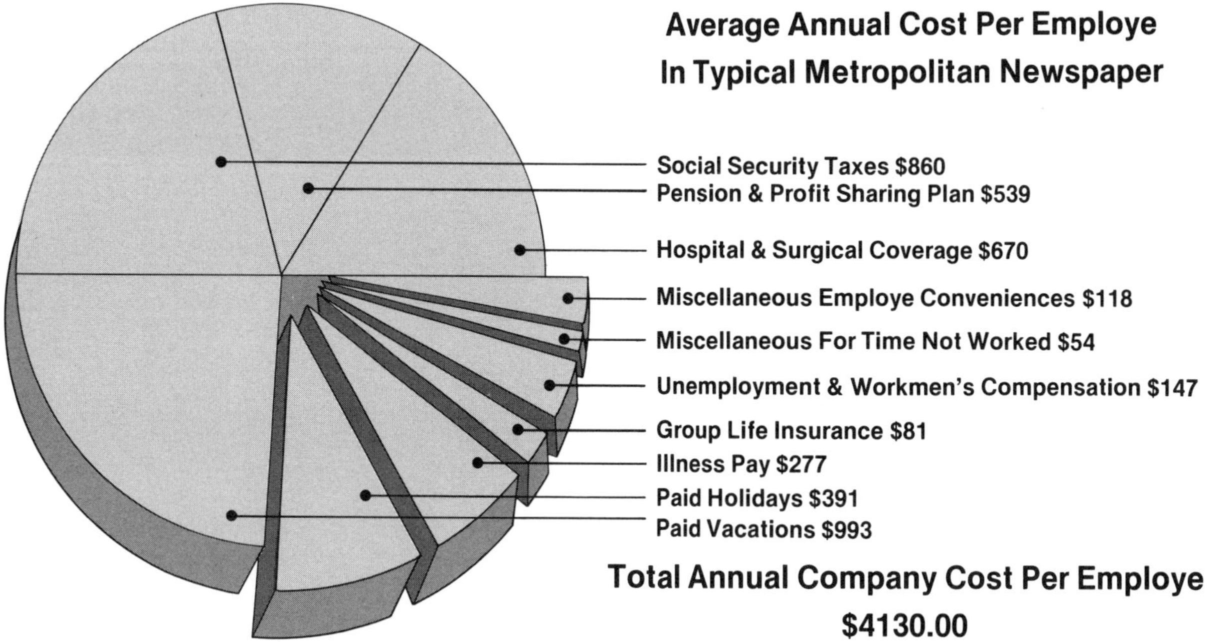

Social Security Taxes $860
Pension & Profit Sharing Plan $539
Hospital & Surgical Coverage $670
Miscellaneous Employe Conveniences $118
Miscellaneous For Time Not Worked $54
Unemployment & Workmen's Compensation $147
Group Life Insurance $81
Illness Pay $277
Paid Holidays $391
Paid Vacations $993

**Total Annual Company Cost Per Employe
$4130.00**

Source: Newspapers, Inc.

Fortunately, there appears to be increasing recognition by top newspaper labor union officers that arbitration is a respectable alternative to strikes. There have been too many instances in past years of tragic, long-term newspaper shutdowns due to strikes by a small percentage of total employes. The public has suffered the loss of its major source of information, merchants have been deprived of their most effective advertising medium, and employes have faced the hardship of long periods without work. Obviously, a newspaper suffers a loss of revenue which cannot be recaptured. Many times it also incurs a permanent loss of circulation.

In the last few years, new production technology has enabled some newspapers to continue publishing even though one employe group may be on strike. During a 1975 pressmen's strike, *The Washington Post* published regularly, although for a time on a curtailed basis. A newspaper's ability to publish in spite of a labor despute somewhat evens the balance at the bargaining table. It tends to motivate both parties to give serious consideration to arbitration as an alternative to strikes.

"People Power" Planning

Personnel planning for the future is an important part of employe relations. An intelligent newspaper management must prepare long and short range people power forecasts, in much the same way as expected sales, revenue, expenses and capital expenditures are planned.

A newspaper employer must be prepared to adjust to changing demographic characteristics and reader interests. The median educational level is moving upward; the average age of the population is shifting. Thirty-five years ago, 52 percent of U.S. families were headed by a blue-collar worker. Today, only 35 percent of all workers hold blue-collar jobs, and most of them are highly skilled. The traditional boundaries that used to separate people on geographical, social, educational, sex, race and income levels have been disappearing gradually.

Obviously, these same changes have affected newspaper work forces. Their educational level is rising; average age is being reduced as older workers can afford to retire at an earlier age. More and more women and racial minorities work for newspapers.

Newspapers have to consider people-power planning to attract, train and retain competent employes to write, edit, produce, promote, distribute and successfully manage the newspaper of tomorrow. A younger and better-educated employe, male or female, looks for new job satisfactions, including growth and challenge. The continuing movement away from individualized craft skills to specialized machine operations in the production process complicates management's challenge. Some highly skilled jobs are being eliminated while new skills are being required. At the same time, the higher educational level, age and sophistication of the average reader calls for specialized writers and news content in a number of different fields. Newspapers should perceive and anticipate these changes in their hiring and training plans.

Management's challenge is to orient all employes, union and nonunion, to their newspaper's basic importance and its vital role in the community being served. Newspapers are increasingly developing educational and communication programs to instill pride in each employe's work. Without pride and performance in every department of the newspaper, the paper cannot achieve its full potential in serving the community.

Employe Benefits

Employes in almost every business have come to expect and take for granted what used to be called "fringe benefits." The dictionary defines fringe as "an ornamental border trimming, an edging or a margin." Certainly that is a misnomer when it is applied to the sizable financial outlays for most newspapers' employe-benefit programs.

Employe benefits range from pension plans to free parking. Most metrpolitan newspapers provide a paid vacation, paid holidays, illness or disability pay, pension program, hospital and surgical coverage for an employe and his or her family, group life insurance and a variety of subsidized employe conveniences such as cafeterias and first aid facilities. Added to these are legally required benefits such as Social Security, unemployment compensation and workmen's compensation insurance for on-the-job injuries. These benefits provide an umbrella of financial security against "rainy day" contingencies during active employment years and a source of continuing income for retirement and leisure-time living.

From the employe relations standpoint, employe benefits are necessary to attract and hold good employes. From a financial standpoint, they can add disproportionately to the cost of operating a business unless they are carefully monitored. For example, the cost of providing an employe and his family with hospital and surgical coverage has more than doubled in recent years; the employer cost for Social Security has increased about 90 percent in just four years. In general, most metropolitan newspapers currently are spending from 20 to 25 percent of total payroll costs for employe benefits.

There is often a tendency simply to keep on adding employe benefits in a haphazard way as they become available. The result is a hodgepodge of costly frills. A high-priced benefit program may be of real value to only 10 percent of all employes. There is a need to provide employe benefits in an integrated package designed to meet the needs of the typical employe. Periodically, the cost of each specific part of the package should be reviewed in relation to the value of the benefit to a majority of employes. As an example, should a newspaper spend $25,000 a year to outfit and maintain a semi-pro employe baseball team if only 2 percent of its employes participate or attend games? Should $10,000 be spent for an annual employe picnic if only 20 percent of the employes really want to attend such an event?

The mounting cost of employe benefits underscores the need for constant review. Dollars spent should provide a well-rounded package of financial protection for the greatest number of employes. Therefore, management has to know employe wants and needs. In addition, employes should be reminded at least annually of benefits provided, their cost and the value of these non-taxable earnings.

Communication

The most important key to effective employe relations can be summarized in one word—communication. The first concept that newspapers should communicate more effectively is the importance of a legally and economically free press in a free society. When the news media come under government control, ownership or subsidy, society itself is threatened. That message needs to be clearly explained and reexplained by newspaper management to its employes and to the general public.

Newspaper employes also should be reminded that real job security can only result from employment in a profitable business. It is conservatively estimated that for every existing job in the newspaper business, an investor had to risk at least $20,000 to provide land, bricks, mortar, machinery, equipment and furniture. It would probably cost at least $3 million today to start a small newspaper employing fewer than 100 people—$30,000 per job. How much return should investors expect on their money? If $30,000 were deposited in a savings and loan association for four or six years, it would return around $2,400 per year in interest, and the deposit would be insured by a U.S. government agency. Should an investor expect a better return if he risks $30,000 in the newspaper business?

Importance of internal communications with employes cannot be over-emphasized. Management can make a serious mistake by assuming:

- Our employees already know *that*.

- They don't really care about *that.*
- *That* is none of their business.

There is little risk of overkill in repetitive employe communications.

Determining the "what" and "how" of employe communications involves management's answer to the question, *"What* would I like to know about the company and its operations if I were doing that job?" In addition, any communication announcing a change will be much more acceptable if it tells "why."

Many techniques are available for accomplishing the "how" of effective employe communications. Employe publications, bulletin boards, public address systems, staff meetings and letters to employes' homes all can be useful. But lower ranking supervisors are the key communicators, because they are the management people who encounter employes most frequently.

Most supervisory training programs emphasize communications skill as an essential element of leadership. However, such skill is of little value if supervisors are not kept informed on a timely basis. As one supervisor said, "How can I feel that I am a part of the management team when the union steward finds out about what is going on before I do?"

Effective employe communication also depends on supervisors not to stifle upward communications from employes. Top management needs to know what employes think and feel about the company, and employes need direct contact with upper management echelons. An occasional plant tour, attendance at a departmental meeting and an announced and meaningful "open door" policy can do much to dispel any notion that top management is insensitive to employe needs and ideas.

Conclusion

The dynamic nature of newspapers and the society they serve increases the importance of effective employe relations. Managing change, especially when many people are involved, is a most difficult task. Planning, communication, fair and effective collective bargaining and compensation programs which recognize *all* work-related employe needs are essential to effective employe relations.

Employe relations are especially important to newspapers because they are labor-intensive. In addition, newspaper-production technology is advancing rapidly. A new product resulting from many individual skills must be produced and delivered each day. In order for these individual efforts to successfully meet community needs, employe motivation and cooperation are required. Employes, from janitor to president, must realize that all their contributions affect newspaper quality.

Each employe should take pride in being an essential part of a free press. Management has an obligation to help all employes recognize their roles, to demonstrate the importance of improving both quality and productivity of their newspaper and to be fair in meeting employe needs.

NOTES
Chapter 9

[1] A more intensive analysis of technological change has been presented in Chapter 6, and future technological changes are discussed in Chapter 10.

10

The Newspaper of the Next Decade

A NEWSPAPER READER of the late 1980s is likely to find that his or her daily newspaper looks very much like that of today. The paper on which it is printed *may* be somewhat lighter and manufactured, at least in part, from materials other than costly wood pulp; pages may be slightly narrower, and typography less crowded and more attractive. Technology is the driving force which will make newspaper changes possible. However, more sophisticated management techniques and better-trained employes also will play an essential role in the free newspaper's future.

The Technological Horizon

So-called experts have predicted the demise of newspapers as we know them since the 1930s; yet the "traditional" newspaper continues to be the nation's largest communication medium in news and editorial content, employment, advertising and sales revenue. On the other hand, the technology necessary to "replace" newspapers as we know them is already decades old. Newspapers have been printed in the home on a small printer controlled by electronic impulses. But traditional newspaper production and distribution methods prevail because the cost of an in-home printer, its maintenance, transmission fees and paper continue to substantially exceed the costs of more traditional methods.

In the 1950s and 1960s television became a major new medium of news and entertainment in the communications business. Newspaper publishers were stimulated to spur development of technology for newspapers.[1] The resulting revolution in newspaper technology has laid the groundwork for substantial further benefits for the future.

Newspapers of the next decade probably will be printed by the same processes available today, but on lighter-weight presses and with more and improved printing-plate options. The shift to offset printing will continue, particularly among small and medium-sized newspapers. Hot metal type-setting machines will be totally replaced by photocomposition and cold type. Laser scanners and laser plate-engravers likely will become an economic alternative to the camera platemaking process.[2] Press plates will be plastic or light-weight metal.

Another printing option, now in development, could eliminate press plates altogether. This process uses computer-controlled ink jets to "spray" the ink onto newsprint. It could lead to a fast, flexible newspaper-printing process that would allow a change of editions without stopping the plateless printing machine.

Application of electronic text-processing, automated typesetting and photosensitive platemaking technologies should improve productivity by at least 10 to 15 percent more.[3]

Computers will play an expanded role, especially in composition and makeup of a newspaper; the entire content of many newspapers may be processed electronically.

On-line display terminals for advertising will simplify the most complex part of newspaper composition, and the computer may provide for complete, electronic full-page assembly. But, the cost of hardware and supporting programs to handle full-page composition may continue to be greater than the cost of the paste-up activity it would replace in most newspapers.

With computers, video-display terminals and other electronic devices, editors will be able to revise copy to meet readers' needs with greater speed and efficiency. While it is possible to install a completely integrated computerized system, minicomputer installations are more likely. Such installations cost less and minimize transition problems.

During the last ten years, small and medium-sized newspapers changed production techniques more than big-city dailies. Large metropolitan newspapers will change the most in the next decade.

Metropolitan newspapers of the late 1980s may have more than one plant. New microwave transmitting technology is enabling newspapers to transmit page images for printing at satellite plants. Such a plant needs no composition facilities, only an offset press. Eventually, newspapers in our largest cities each may have three or four satellite presses located strategically throughout their distribution areas. Satellite pressrooms may be used to print other newspapers as well. A suburban paper, for example, could publish without building its own press facility, and a metropolitan paper could make greater use of its pressroom capcacity. Big papers could start their own suburban shoppers.

Advancing technology will do more than change composition and printing processes. It will enhance newspapers' economic viability through increased efficiency. Production personnel will enjoy more sophisticated jobs with less drudgery and better working conditions. Advertisers will have greater flexibility in using the newspaper medium for delivery of their messages. Perhaps most significant, readers may find newspaper content better oriented to their individual needs and desires. Computers and satellite press locations will make it economically feasible to produce special editions catering to specific urban or suburban locations. While special sections or editions will add to newspaper costs and circulation and advertising rates, newspapers will have greater value to readers and advertisers.

These exciting developments are already occurring. *The Minneapolis Star and Tribune* has installed the first full-page pagination system, and will be among the first newspapers in the world without a composing room.[4] *The Wall Street Journal* transmits its entire Florida edition from Massachusetts to Florida via domestic satellite, making it possible to run the entire Florida plant with just 19 people.[5] The ANPA Research Institute is spearheading the perfection of low cost microwave receivers that can fit on the roof of a newspaper plant to receive information from a satellite instead of telephone lines. This could lead to a nationwide satellite microwave communications network for newspapers, bypassing traditional telephone cables and towers. Not only would such a system offer economic advantages, it would provide a nationwide system for instantaneous transmission of advertising and editorial messages.

While the promise is great, a caveat is in order. Advancing technology, in and of itself, does not guarantee new efficiency, better newspapers or improved profit. Technology must be wisely managed to be beneficial. Newspaper management must analyze carefully its needs, evaluate advances in light of those needs and train appropriate personnel to use the new tools which are adopted. Without a cautious and carefully managed approach, new technology can bring confusion and dissention between management and employes, increase costs and destroy customer and employe goodwill. *Advanced technology is merely a tool which must be selected and used wisely.*

Converting a newspaper from old systems and processes to all the latest available technology in a new plant challenges even the best managers. Many employes must develop entirely new skills; some skills become totally obsolete. Training and personnel problems usually are horrendous. Before employes iron out bugs in new equipment and processes, printing errors, delayed press runs and a poor-quality product often cause customer dissatisfaction and conflicts within the newspaper family. Technological advances constitute progress only when well managed.

The Physical Product

In the last 20 years newspapers have gone through several format changes, largely dictated by periodic shortages and skyrocketing prices of newsprint. Faced with a need to conserve paper, publishers moved toward narrower pages and rediscovered readability formulas showing that somewhat longer lines are easier to read. This led many papers to a six-column page or one of its many variations.

Many advertising sizing problems already have been ameliorated through standards which enable advertisers to produce their materials in a minimum number of variations. Technology—such as computer composition—will make it possible in the future for advertisers and editors to arrange their material in almost any format desired, and space communications could enable newspapers to swiftly receive both advertising and news via satellite-signal direct to the newspaper plant.

Newsprint conservation will continue as prices rise and shortages occur because of surges in demand, delays in mill capacity expansion and occasional mill or railroad strikes. For publishers, however, emphasis will be on efficient newsprint use. Newsprint consumption will continue to increase, as waste reductions are outweighed by newspaper growth and increased paper consumption for specialized editions or sections to serve diverse reader desires. Research efforts will focus on finding new newsprint-production technology so that new, lightweight newsprint machines may ultimately be located nearer both newspapers and new fiber-crop pulp sources.

The 1980s will be a transition period from essentially one edition for all readers to the twenty-first century basic edition supplemented by specialized sections or editions for various major segments of the population. Electronic composition and satellite printing will make product differentiation practical—to the benefit of readers, advertisers and publishers alike. A news story or an advertisement with general interest will continue to appear in the basic paper. Those of special interest to certain readers only will appear in specialized sections or editions which go to those readers.

Advertising and Competition

In the next decade new technology will make the newspaper a more sophisticated and widely used advertising medium. Technology will make it easier for a newspaper to adopt the "marketing concept" in selling advertising. Advertising personnel will be better able to coordinate with other divisions to group advertising with related news and special features. Some newspapers will be able to offer their full circulation to those advertisers wanting to reach the entire public, and "split" runs for those seeking to reach only identifiable segments of a newspaper's audience, such as readers in a specific geographic area. Computer text-processing, with ads sorted and formatted by a computer, will make it possible to accept and typeset advertisements within an hour of press time. This will allow a newspaper to offer its advertisers more timely changes in their advertising keyed to the weather or unexpected news events.

Thousands of small retailers today do not use metropolitan newspaper advertising because the involved circulation extends far beyond their trading areas. To the extent that newspaper specialization occurs, it will provide new marketing opportunities for these retailers. They will be able to place their advertisements in the edition of the daily newspaper which primarily reaches their potential customers. Similarly, readers will appreciate receiving more local shopping information. Specialization represents substantial potential for newspaper advertising growth in the years ahead.

The same techniques also will be applied to classified advertising. For many years virtually all classified advertising has been "full run" in all copies or editions of a daily newspaper because it was too expensive to pull out small ads and "remake" pages. Computer technology will make it possible to offer classified advertising on the same split-run basis. This will be particularly useful to small retailers and service shops and will increase classified advertising's readership and value. While the advertising rate per copy distributed will be higher for split than full runs, the rate per potential customer reached will be considerably lower.

The newspaper will continue to be the major medium for classified advertising. The broadcast media simply cannot serve this market because of a lack of time. Also, the typical classified advertiser cannot afford broadcast rates.

The electronic media's only real opportunity to reach specialized segments of the population is through cable systems. However, glowing predictions for the cable have not and are not likely to materialize during the next decade. The cost of cable systems has increased greatly and cable operators are restricted by federal, state and local regulations and must pay exorbitant charges to some municipalities for the right to operate. Cable restrictions may be loosened, but cable will remain largely a supplement to television. Even if successful, cable television is unlikely to attract a large volume of advertising because the large number of stations and proliferation of television channels would fragment the viewing audience, tending to make newspapers more attractive for general audience advertising.

Also boosting newspaper advertising are expanding state and federal rulings concerning television advertising and sales techniques. Already the federal government prohibits cigarette advertising on radio and television, and requires certain factual information in advertisements for some products and services. Additional restrictions promise to make it increasingly difficult for some advertisers to prepare broadcast sales messages. If certain facts are legally required in an advertisement, an advertiser will need to purchase additional broadcast time or reduce the promotional content of the advertising message. Frequently, only printed media offer enough space to economically present a full story in a single advertisement while meeting government requirements.

Television's share of advertising revenues appears to be stabilizing; it is no longer rising at a rapid pace. Newspapers should, therefore, enjoy a greater growth rate. Their competitive position may also be enhanced by economic advantages. As pointed out in a study by Arthur D. Little, "The newspaper industry in the next 10 years will deal successfully with inflationary forces and improve its cost performance and competitive position relative to competing advertising media (TV and magazines)."[6] Because of productivity increases and better managerial controls made possible by emerging technology, newspaper ad rates are expected to remain low enough to capture a larger share of the advertising dollar.

However, the competition for advertising dollars will continue to be intense and television will continue to push the expansion of local spot advertising. Because of the rising diversity of life styles, the media are becoming increasingly fragmented. For example, the tennis buff is more likely to purchase a tennis magazine than mass appeal magazines such as *Life* and *Look*, which have now disappeared from the marketplace.

The trend toward fragmentation will have a mixed impact on community newspapers. While fragmentation tends to adversely affect general interest media, the community newspaper has survived because of its wide range of content which includes something for almost every interest group. Therefore, it continues to be one of the few media reaching many specialized interest groups *and* a wide general audience. This capability should favor the growth of newspaper advertising.

News-Editorial Competition

It is in the arena of news-editorial competition that a newspaper of the next decade will face one of its stiffest challenges. Based on public opinion polls—with the same questions used year after year—newspapers have declined in public esteem, both as a prime source of news and as a believable medium.

Ironically, adoption of new production technology has sometimes impacted reader confidence. Many newspapers installed new composition equipment before all the bugs had been ironed out, and produced a plethora of typographical errors. New computerized composition and makeup systems, properly programmed, will produce fewer typographical errors.

Measured by most opinion polls, public trust in the accuracy of news reporting in all media is too low for editors' tastes. Many newspapers have been attacking the "credibility" problem through a variety of techniques. Several papers have appointed ombudsmen to hear and act on reader complaints. Many publish columns or feature articles explaining problems of news coverage, and many more regularly run corrections of errors in news stories. Future editorial success of newspapers will depend in great measure on newspaper efforts to improve accuracy, to communicate with readers, to inspire confidence in the accuracy of news columns and to convey a sense of fairness and even friendliness on every page.

The news content of large newspapers probably will be of more interest to readers in the future because of specialized sections for neighborhoods or "interest profiles." However, readers will recognize inaccuracies even more readily than today because they are likely to be even more knowledgeable about topics which interest them.

In competition with other media, a newspaper should have an advantage in reader appeal. Its basic edition will cover international, national and local news of interest to the general reader. Specialized editions and sections will fill out news packages for readers in various interest groups.

Like newspaper advertising, newspaper editorial content is not subject to broadcasting's time limits. This is an enormous competitive advantage, particularly since a newspaper of the future will need to be increasingly tailored to comprehensively meet the needs of diverse readership groups. Displays of factual text and competing opinions are possible on a television screen, but not in any comprehensive way during the foreseeable future.

In much of its content the newspaper will be a medium of explanation. It will have moderated the historic emphasis on being first with spot news, recognizing that broadcast media have an inherent time advantage. But, investigative "scoops" will continue to be a newspaper's preserve. And, a newspaper has sufficient space to explain the background and details of an event, relate it to other events or pending developments and present commentaries from a wide variety of knowledgable persons.

At the same time, the newspaper of the future will have an improved capacity to report news quickly. Portable remote terminals have been developed which allow a reporter to prepare copy in the field on the keyboard of a device which rapidly can transmit copy directly to a newsroom computer by telephone. This advance, coupled with rapid composition and typesetting systems, will permit a story which breaks near press time to be published almost as rapidly as it is broadcast, but in far more detail. Some day the remote terminal will also handle still pictures.

The future editor's control of a newspaper's content and appearance probably will be firmer than today. Because of computerized data banks of information and of travelling reporters equipped to transmit stories directly to the newsroom, editors will have a wider selection of stories from which to choose. In addition, editorial affiliations may develop within newspaper groups or among independents which will provide whole sections, pages or inserts on a timely basis which are shared via satellite or microwave transmission in much the same way that wire service material is shared today.

Looking to the twenty-first century, newspapers will be marketing a wide variety of information which they now discard. This will take several different forms. Each day a newspaper receives many times as much information as it can publish. In the future, news from wire services will be digitally encoded in computers, ready for manipulation into packages of data useful to special interest groups such as sports enthusiasts, business people and homemakers. Such packages could take the form of local specialized publications issued weekly or more frequently.

Distribution

Of all the elements of newspaper operations, distribution presents the most nagging problems. No other industry creates and delivers such a complex product on a daily basis, or even tries to deliver such a modestly-priced item on such a rigid time schedule. In most cases home delivery is no more expensive to a reader than buying a single copy at a newsstand. Furthermore, final delivery usually still depends on a boy or girl. This delivery system has been a great success and is

152 □ The Economics of the American Newspaper

unlikely to be discarded during the next decade. However, major changes will be well underway by that time.

New ideas for newspaper distribution are being tried. The newspaper "mail" room already is partially automated, but more automation will come, particularly for insertion of special sections and preprinted advertising supplements into the basic paper.

New ideas for truck routing from the plant to distribution points are being tried, including the use of large trucks where a major traffic artery makes it feasible. This involves trucking to a distribution center from which many smaller trucks can depart without getting into midtown traffic. New types of energy-efficient trucks will be developed and used.

A newspaper with satellite printing plants around the rim of the core city will have fewer distribution problems at least from plant to distribution center. But juvenile carriers dislike early morning delivery and periodic collecting at night. More adults will be carriers. Also, most newspapers will use computers to bill all subscribers for direct payment, relieving carriers of the collecting chore.

Unfortunately, even a modern distribution system may not always help newspapers reach urban apartment dwellers and persons in high-crime, central-city areas. Security measures in some apartment complexes make it difficult for carriers to gain admittance. Despite the current economic disadvantages of in-home printers, some metropolitan newspapers eventually may utilize them—or even video cassettes—for reaching subscribers in locations where the carrier system is not feasible.

Newsprint Supply

Future U.S. newspaper growth depends upon adequate newsprint supply. Historically, periodic shortages have limited newspaper expansion. For example, in 1973 strikes in Canada greatly reduced the flow of paper to the United States. After the strikes, supply expanded but at a substantially higher price.

However, newspapers do have a major resource advantage—they utilize a renewable and recyclable resource—fiber pulp—which in the future may include both wood pulp and pulp from other, faster growing plants. In addition, newsprint weight can be reduced further to conserve the pulp resource. By the late 1980s most U.S. newspapers may be using 28-pound newsprint as opposed to 30-pound in 1975 and 32-pound in 1965. Today, European newspapers rapidly are adapting to newsprint equivalent to a 27.7-pound weight.

Most U.S. newspapers are currently unable to economically use the

27.7-pound newsprint because over 60 percent of U.S. paper supply comes from Canada, and U.S. tariffs are charged on newsprint with less than a 28.5-pound basis weight. This legal barrier to economic use of lighter weight newsprint probably will be repealed in the next decade, particularly if paper manufacturing technology improves the quality of lighter newsprint.

Meanwhile, improved forest management will ensure that trees used for paper-making are harvested only in replaceable quantities. And new technology may make non-wood-fiber newsprint economical.

A newsprint mill which will use sugar cane stalks (bagasse) for pulp is under construction in South America. The American Newspaper Publishers Association Research Institute is studying newsprint made of "kenaf" a farm product which can be grown in most areas of North America. Also, used newsprint is and will be recycled. While most recycled newsprint today is used for paperboard or other products such as insulation, an increasing proportion is being de-inked and used again to make newsprint.

Economics

The major economic problem for newspapers during the next decade is inflation. The cost of labor and materials will continue to rise, forcing up advertising and circulation rates. However, emerging technology and improved management methods will help slow the rise of production costs. Productivity gains will occur primarily in pre-press production operations as a result of improved information-handling and typesetting systems. More efficient press operations, page formats and careful control will save newsprint. The latest information on street sales and subscriptions will be used to set press runs and reduce "overruns."

As a result of increased efficiency, newspaper costs and prices *may* not rise as fast as those of competitive industries. However, large newspapers will not achieve a competitive advantage without increasing distribution efficiency. That efficiency may depend on advancing data transmission technology and satellite printing operations. Newspapers will continue to enjoy a rapid growth of preprinted advertising inserts by being able to deliver the inserts more cheaply than bulk-rate mail or other delivery systems.

Newspaper Employes

As a place to work, the newspaper is likely to become even more attractive than it is today. The hot-metal production facility of the past has been described as a combination of a dungeon and a blacksmith shop, with the added discomforts of ink mists and loud noise. Conditions will be greatly improved during the next ten years.

New technology already has eliminated much drudgery in the production process. Future advances will bring about a more efficient, quiet, safer operation from preparation of news and advertising copy to final printing. In the old days newspaper production employes had to wear work clothes and wash up before going home. By the late 1980s many production workers will dress more like today's doctors and business executives.

News and advertising employes will find their work highly integrated with the production process. Original news and advertising copy will flow—without re-keyboarding—through editing, proofreading, page assembly and printing, with other employes controlling the process with computers and video display terminals.

Editors will have greater control of a newspaper's content and appearance. They will have a wider selection of national and regional material from which to choose. More photographs will be transmitted, and they will be of improved quality. Better national telecommunications facilities and satellite communications systems around the world will support an expanded data transmission system, perhaps at lower costs than today.

A new category of employes will emerge, probably managed by the editorial department. They will be responsible for computer and electronic systems.

Most newspapers will have more traveling reporters, each equipped with a remote terminal for transmission of news stories. Locally, the reporter will continue to be the eyes and ears of the newspaper. A reporter will be dispatched, as now, by an editor. He or she will gather the news, but will not necessarily have to return to the main plant to prepare his story. The typical reporter may use an on-line portable typewriter. With software support it will be possible for the reporter to backspace and strike out as he or she types, and read the story in its final form as it is filed in the data base. Where computer support is not available, a reporter's typewriter will "output" to a cassette. The cassette story then will be read into the data base without sophisticated computer support.

During the next decade there will be greater emphasis on technical and managerial expertise in all newspaper departments. A smaller percentage of the workforce will be production workers, but they will be better paid than today. Coordination will be essential, with news and advertising personnel required to understand and participate more in the production process than they do today. There will be substantial use of the "marketing" or "total newspaper" concept. The importance of marketing will rise as newspapers adjust to the increasingly dynamic society.

A Long-Term Economic Threat

The growth and prosperity of a newspaper is highly correlated with the economics of the community it serves. Therefore, the greatest threat to newspapers and to the free press of the future is possible stagnation of the U.S. economy or the communities which many newspapers serve. Inflation continues to be an "economic cancer" which destroys healthy economic cells in the economic system it ravages. Fortunately, some progress has been made in the battle against inflation.

Conclusion

From the turn of the century until the 1960s, methods of producing the American newspaper remained virtually unchanged. However, few industries have greeted massive technological change as enthusiastically as today's newspapers. As a result, the newspaper of the next decade should easily survive all competitive challenges from other media.

More important, newspapers will perform their constitutional, public-service role more effectively than ever before. Readers will find their familiar-appearing newspapers to be even better and more useful sources of news and advertising information.

As publishers and editors acknowledge their own weaknesses and take steps to correct them, the public will gain further confidence in the press as a source of objective information. With this continued public acceptance free newspapers will play their indispensible role in a free society—during the next decade, and for so long as a free society thrives.

NOTES
Chapter 10

[1] For a discussion of this historical development see Chapter 6.
[2] Arthur D. Little, *Threats and Opportunities Within the Newsprint—Newspaper Industry*, Cambridge, Mass., October 1974, Part I, p. 17.
[3] *Ibid.*, p. 18.
[4] Robert G. Marbut, "Newspaper Technology: Today and Tomorrow," Congress of the International Federation of Newspaper Publishers, Bologna, Italy, June 1, 1976.
[5] *Ibid.*
[6] Arthur D. Little, *Threats and Opportunities Within the Newsprint-Newspaper Industry*, Part III, December 1974.

Index

Advertising, 26, 28-31, 45-47, 57, 58-59, 82, 84, 92; classified, 110-11, 115-16, 148; cooperative, 114; display, 111; and editorial department, contribution to, 59; growth of newspaper, and U.S. economy, 29, 30-31; local, 110, 111-13; national, 110, 114-15; in quality newspaper, 82; in newspapers of next decade, 147, 148-49; as reader service, 58-59; revenues from, *see* Advertising revenue; shares of, by major media, 30-31; zoned, 112, 113, 116*n*.

Advertising revenue, 108-16; and circulation, 109; from classified advertising, 115-16; competition for, by various media, 110; from local retail advertising, 111-13; and management policies, 109; and market, relationship to, 108-09; from national advertising, 114-15; from preprints, 111

Age of Discontinuity, The (Drucker), 69

America, Inc. (Mintz and Cohen), 76

American Newspaper Publishers Association (ANPA), 34, 51, 55, 90, 94, 115, 146, 153

American Press Institute, 49

American Society of Newspaper Editors (ASNE), 24

Anderson, Roy W., 127

Associated Press Managing Editors Association, 54

Audit Bureau of Circulation, 45

Automated typesetting, 145

Backup equipment, for new technology, 97

Bagasse, 153

Bagdikian, Ben, 65

Balanced news presentation, 81

Bill of Rights, 14

Boston Globe, The, 126

Bradlee, Benjamin C., 66

Cable television, 148-49

Californian, The, 66

Canada, 152, 153
Capital: profit as compensation for, 68-69; required for converting to new technology, 95-98; return on, 71-72
Capital formation, 19
Carnegie, Andrew, 18
Cassette, "output" to, from reporter's typewriter, 154
Cathode Ray Tube (CRT), 94
Chandler, Otis, 66, 73, 75
Chapman, Alvah H., Jr., 75
Charlotte (N.C.) *Observer,* 76
Chicago Day Book, 41
China, 17
Circulation revenue, 100-08; and dealers, 100; and distributors, independent, 100, 101; effect of prices on, 103-06; and "little merchants," 100, 101; from mail subscriptions, 101; and opportunities and problems, 107-08; and prices, effect of, 103-06; and pricing practices, 102; and problems and opportunities, 107-08; trends in, 101-02; from vendingbox sales, 101
Cleghorn, Reese, 76
Cohen, Jerry S., 76
Colburn, John, 66
Cold type, 94, 98*n*.
Commerce Department, U.S., 30
Compensatory theory of profit, 67, 68
Computer, 46, 87, 89, 94, 95, 96, 97, 145, 146, 147, 148, 150, 151, 152, 154
Constitution, U.S., 13, 14, 21
Constitutional Convention, 15
Consumerism, 18
Cost per 1000 (CPM) data, 115
Costs, operating, of newspapers, *see* Operating costs of newspapers
Credit-card charging, for newspaper sales, 101
Crime, urban, 31, 152

Declaration of Independence, 13
Democracy, American, economics of, 13-21 *passim*
Depreciation of equipment, for tax purposes, 97-98
Di-Litho TM, 95
Distributors, independent, 100, 101

Dow Jones & Company, Inc., 65
Drucker, Peter, 19, 69, 126
Dunleavy, Edward, 70

Economic system: competition in, 18, 21; government's role in, 20-21; and individualism, 17; and newspapers, 16, 18, 21; profit motive in, 18-20; *see also* Free enterprise; Free market
Electronic technology for newspaper production, 89, 93-95, 145, 146, 147, 148, 154; capital requirements for, 95-98
Employee relations in newspaper business, 131-43, 153-55; and collective bargaining, 137; communication as key to effective, 141-42; and compensation, 136; and employee benefits, 138, 140-41; importance of, 132-33; and "people power" planning, 139-40; and unionization, 132, 137
Engman, Lewis, 21
Exploitation-of-labor theory of profit, 67, 68

Federal Communications Commission, 77
Federal Trade Commission, 21, 70
Federalists, 15
Fiber pulp, 152
Fifth Amendment, 14
First Amendment, 13, 14, 16, 23, 54, 64, 66
Ford, Henry, 18
Ford Motor Company, 17
Free enterprise, 16-21 *passim*, 65; defined, 16; and profits, 66, 67; *see also* Economic system; Free market
Free market, 15, 21; consumer choice in, 17-18; profit motive in, 18-20; *see also* Economic system; Free enterprise
Free press, 13, 14, 16, 17, 21, 41, 48, 76, 155
Friction and monopoly theory of profit, 67, 68

Gannett Company, 76, 77, 128
Gross national product (GNP), 28, 36

158 □ **Index**

Growth of newspapers, 38; in cities, 38; in geographic regions, 37; vs. national growth, 34-36

Hamilton, Alexander, 15
Hard copy, 92, 94
Harte-Hanks Communications, Inc., 64, 127
Hecht, Ben, 133
Hynds, Ernest, 75

Individualism, and free enterprise, 17
Inflation, 73, 74, 102, 117, 124, 149, 153, 155
Ink jets, computer-controlled, 95, 145
Innovation theory of profit, 67, 68
International Typographical Union, 132
Interstate Commerce Commission, 21

Jefferson, Thomas, 15; quoted, 13
Justice Department, U.S., 77

Kenaf, 153
Knight-Ridder newspapers, 75, 76
Kraft, Joseph, 55

Labor relations, *see* Employee relations in newspaper business
Laser plate-engraver, 145
Laser scanner, 145
Letterpress, 96, 97
Life magazine, 149
Little, Arthur D., 149
"Little merchant plan" for newspaper distribution, 100, 101
Look magazine, 149
Los Angeles Times, The, 66, 124, 132
Louisville Courier-Journal, 129

Madison, James, 15
Marbut, Robert G., 64, 127
Market, free, *see* Free market
Marx, Karl, 68
Meany, George, 77
Mercantilism, 14-15
Mergenthaler, Ottmar, 88

Merrill Lynch, Pierce, Fenner and Smith, 70, 112
Miami Herald, The, 132
Microwave transmission, 89, 145, 146
Milwaukee Journal, The, 84
Milwaukee Journal Company, 76
Milwaukee Journal/Sentinel, The, 107
Milwaukee Sentinel, The, 76
Minneapolis Star and Tribune, The, 146
Mintz, Morton, 76
Morton, John, 70

Nader, Ralph, 21
Needham, James, 69
Neuharth, Allen, 77
New York Herald-Tribune, The, 80
New York Times, The, 132
New York Stock Exchange, 69
News American, The, 127
News hole, 122
Newspaper Advertising Bureau, 24
Newspaper Format Committee, ANPA, 115
Newspaper Guild, 132
Newspaper Preservation Act, 71
Newspapers: and accuracy of news reporting, 150; advertising in: *see* Advertising; Advertising revenue; and changes in market, 50-51; circulation of, 31-34, 43-44, 45, 59-60, 102-08, 109 (*see also* Circulation revenue); and competition of other media, 148-51; and consensus, social, 53-57; costs and cost control of, *see* Operating costs of newspapers; credibility problem of, 150; distribution of, new ideas for, 152; dynamics of production of, 88-98; economic status of, 23-38; editorial function of, importance of, 58; electronic technology for production of, *see* Electronic technology for newspaper production; and employee relations, *see* Employee relations in newspaper business; as employers, major, 26, 27; and equity, return on, 70, 71, 72; and free enterprise, 16, 18, 21; group ownership of, 75-77; growth of, *see* Growth of newspapers; home delivery of, 43-44, 100, 101, 102, 151-52; income of, 26 (*see also* Ad-

vertising revenue; Circulation revenue); as labor-intensive business, 133; of late 1980s, 144-55; and marketing concept, 40-62 *passim;* and news reporting, accuracy of, 150; newsstand sales of, 43, 44; of 1980s, late, 144-55; number of, 25, 69; objectivity of, and market-oriented operations, 41, 42; ombudsmen appointed by, 150; organizational structure of, 47-50; prices of, rising, 118; production of, dynamics of, 88-98; and productivity, 125, 126, 136, 137, 149, 153; and profit, understanding of, 64-77 (*see also* Profit); profitability of, 66, 69-70, 71, 73 (*see also* Profit); public ownership of, 74-75; quality, *see* Quality newspapers; and reader interests, determination of, 42-43, 61; and return on equity, 70, 71, 72; revenues of: *see* Advertising revenue; Circulation revenue; salaries and wages paid by, 136; and social consensus, 53-57; social significance of, 23-25; structure of, organizational, 47-50; wages and salaries paid by, 136; youth readership of, 107; *see also* Press

Newsprint: cost of, 73, 102, 118, 120, 124, 125; efficient use of, 147; non-wood-fiber, 153; recycled, 153; supply of, 152-53

Offset printing, 89-90, 94, 95, 96, 145
Ombudsmen, 150
Opelousas (La.) *Daily World,* 90
Operating costs of newspapers, 117-29; and communications, 128; and contingency planning, 128-29; control of, strategies for, 121-29; and coordination of planning, 128; direct fixed, 118, 120; editorial, 122-24; fixed, 118, 120; indirect fixed, 118, 120; measurability of, 127-28; nature of, 118; news-editorial, 122-24; for newsprint, 73, 102, 118, 120, 124, 125; for personnel, 124-27, 138; problems in controlling, 120-21; and productivity, 125, 126; strategies for control of, 121-29; variable, 118

Opinion Research Corporation, 67
Optical Character Reader (OCR), 93-94, 96, 98
Overview of the Newspaper Industry (1975), 112

Penney, J. C., 18
Personnel relations, *see* Employee relations in newspaper business
Phillips, Warren H., 65
Photocomposition, 94, 95, 96, 97, 121
Photoengraving, 93
Plateless printing, 95, 145
PM, 41
Portable remote terminal, 151
Pravda, 17
Preprints (advertising supplements), 111, 153
Press: free, 13, 14, 16, 17, 21, 41, 48, 76, 155; profit problems of, 73-74; *see also* Newspapers
Prime market area, 124
Productivity in newspaper business, 125, 126, 136, 137, 149, 153
Profit: blessings and evils of, 67; as compensation for capital, 68-69; controversy over, 64-66; as cost, 67, 68-69; explanations of, 67-68; reasonable, for newspapers, 72-73; role of, 66
Profit motive, 18-20
Property rights, 14, 17
Pulp, fiber, 152

Quality newspapers: advertising in, 82; appearance of, physical, 82-83; budgeting and planning for, 84-86; community involvement of, 83; delivery service by, 83; editorial opinions of, 82, 83; elements of, 80-83; features of, 81-82; monitoring performance of, 86-87; news content of, 81, 83; performance of, measures of, 86-87; physical appearance of, 82-83; planning and budgeting for, 84-86; pricing, 83-84
Quinn, John C., 76

Radio, 30, 71, 88, 110, 115, 149
Remote terminal, portable, 151

Research Institute, ANPA, 90, 94, 146, 153
Robinson, Claude, 67
Rockefeller, John D., 18
Rotary press, 93, 95

St. Louis Post-Dispatch, 96
Sandburg, Carl, 41
Satellite presses, 146, 152, 153
Schwartz, Harold, 107
Science Management Corporation, 126
Securities and Exchange Commission, 70
Simmons, W. R., 33
Skidmore, James A., 126
Smith, Adam, 13, 15
Socialism, and concept of profit, 20
Soviet Union, 17, 19
Stereotype plates, 93, 94
Stock Exchange, New York, 69
Subscriptions: mail, 101; prepaid, for carrier delivery, 101
Suburbs, flight to, 31
Supplements, newspaper (preprints), 111, 153

Taylor, Arthur R., 65
Taylor, William O., 126
Technology, electronic, for newspaper production, *see* Electronic technology for newspaper production
Television, 30, 31, 71, 88, 89, 106, 110, 114, 115, 116, 145, 149; cable, 148-49
Times Mirror Company, 66, 73, 75
Typesetting, automated, 145
Typewriter, electric, 93, 94, 96, 97
Typographical Union, International, 132

Understanding Profits (Robinson), 67
Unions, 132, 137

Video Display Terminal (VDT), 94, 96, 97, 98, 145

Wall Street Journal, The, 62, 65, 146
Washington Post, The, 66, 139
Wealth of Nations, The (Smith), 13

Yugoslavia, 20

WITHDRAWN
UST
Libraries

```
PN 4734 .U3
Udell, Jon G.
The economics of the
  American newspaper
```

DATE DUE

Demco Inc. 38-293